NATIVE AMERICAN RELIGIONS

WORLD RELIGIONS

by
Paula R. Hartz

☑® Facts On File, Inc.

NATIVE AMERICAN RELIGIONS
World Religions

Facts On File, Inc.
11 Penn Plaza
New York NY 10001

Library of Congress Cataloging-in-Publication Data
Hartz, Paula R.
    Native American Religions / Paula R. Hartz.
        p. cm. — (World Religions)
    Includes bibliographical references and index.
    Summary: surveys the history and basic beliefs of Native American religions.
        ISBN-0-8160-3578-4
        1. Indians of North America—Religion—Juvenile literature.
        2. Indians of North America—Rites and ceremonies—Juvenile literature.
        [1. Indians of North America—Religion. 2. Indians of North America—
    Rites and ceremonies.]
        1. Title. II. Series.
E98.R31125   1997
299'.7—dc21   96-39201

Developed by Brown Publishing Network, Inc. Series Design by Trelawney Goodell.
Design Production by Diana Maloney/Brown Publishing Network, Inc. Photo Research by Nina Whitney.

Photo credits:
Cover: Yei (pronounced "yay") rugs show stylized figures of yei, the supernatural Holy People who carry the prayers of the Navajo to the higher powers of the universe. The yei figures are adapted from those that appear in Navajo sand painting designs, which are created as part of Navajo ritual and considered too sacred to be reproduced. Although they depict sacred figures, yei rugs are not sacred and are not used in ceremonies. Traditional Navajo, however, still consider any depiction of the yei for anything other than ritual purposes to be controversial. George H.H. Huey; *Title page:* Participant in the opening ceremony of a powwow offers a prayer. Steve Bly; *Table of Contents page:* Wallowa Lake and Mountains in Oregon are sacred spots for Native American vision quests. Courtesy of the Oregon Tourist Commission; 7 Stephen Trimble; 15 Steve Bly; 16 Jerry Jack; 20 Stephen Trimble; 23 Ted Wood; 25 Jerry Jacka; 28 Steve Bly; 30 Corbis-Bettmann; 33 Lawrence Migdale; 41 Dave G. Houser; 45 Smithsonian Institution; 49 Jerry Jacka; 51 UPI/Corbis-Bettmann; 53 UPI/Corbis-Bettmann, 55 Stephen Trimble; 60 Stephen Trimble; 64 Ted Wood; 67 Corbis-Bettmann; 69 Ted Wood; 79 Jerry Jacka; 82 Jerry Jacka; 84 Stephen Trimble; 87 Elliott Smith; 93 Elliott Smith; 97 Stephen Trimble; 109 Corbis-Bettmann; 111 Ted Wood; 116 Corbis-Bettmann.

TABLE OF CONTENTS

Preface   4

CHAPTER 1   Introduction: The Sacred Way   6

CHAPTER 2   The Spirit World and the Sacred Way   16

CHAPTER 3   Creating the World: The Oral Tradition   32

CHAPTER 4   Native American Ceremonies and Rituals   48

CHAPTER 5   Wholeness and Healing   64

CHAPTER 6   The Path of Life   78

CHAPTER 7   Native American Religions and Christianity   92

CHAPTER 8   Native American Religions Today   110

Glossary   121

Chapter Notes   124

For Further Reading   124

Index   125

Preface

The twentieth century is sometimes called a "secular age," meaning, in effect, that religion is not an especially important issue for most people. But there is much evidence to suggest that this is not true. In many societies, including the United States, religion and religious values shape the lives of millions of individuals and play a key role in politics and culture as well.

The World Religions series, of which this book is a part, is designed to appeal to both students and general readers. The books offer clear, accessible overviews of the major religious traditions and institutions of our time. Each volume in the series describes where a particular religion is practiced, its origins and history, its central beliefs and important rituals, and its contributions to world civilization. Carefully chosen photographs complement the text, and a glossary and bibliography are included to help readers gain a more complete understanding of the subject at hand.

Religious institutions and spirituality have always played a central role in world history. These books will help clarify what religion is all about and reveal both the similarities and differences in the great spiritual traditions practiced around the world today.

Areas where Native American religions can be found

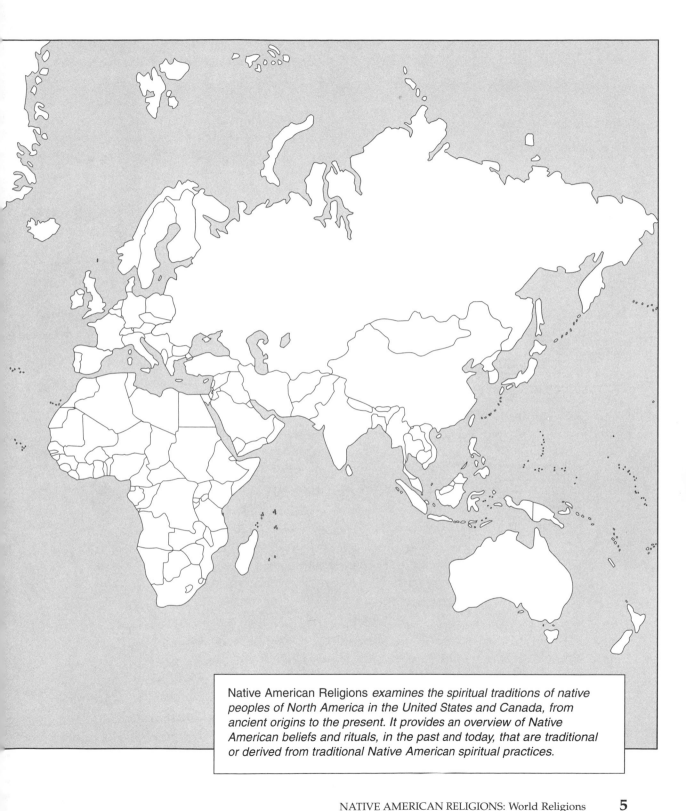

Native American Religions *examines the spiritual traditions of native peoples of North America in the United States and Canada, from ancient origins to the present. It provides an overview of Native American beliefs and rituals, in the past and today, that are traditional or derived from traditional Native American spiritual practices.*

CHAPTER 1

Introduction:
The Sacred Way

*E*ach year in June, when the sun is highest in the sky, holy men of the Lakota of the western Plains choose a special sacred place in the countryside. The area, which changes every year, must be large and open, away from buildings that detract from the purity of the landscape. Sagebrush and cottonwood trees must grow nearby. When the holy men have chosen a site, they perform the complex rituals necessary to sanctify the land for the Sun Dance, a Lakota ceremony for world renewal.

At the appointed time, hundreds of members of the Lakota people, many of whom have traveled great distances for the ceremony, gather at the site to participate in or observe the four-day ritual of the Sun Dance. In the Lakota religion, people understand themselves to be a part of the cycle of all life. The Sun Dance reminds them of their sacred origins and the necessity of living in harmony with the rhythms of the earth to maintain balance and order in the universe. It is an important part of Lakota culture, one of seven sacred ceremonies that the Lakota believe were brought to their people by Buffalo Calf Woman, a spirit messenger.

Traditional Homelands of Major Native American Groups ca.1700–1800s

Northwest Coast
(Above the Columbia River, along the Pacific Coast to southern Alaska)

Bella Bella
Bella Coola
Chinook
Coast Salish:
  Chehallis
  Nisqually
  Puyallup
  Quinanet
Eyah
Haida
Kwakiutl
Nootka
Quileute
Tillamook
Tlingit
Tsimshian

California
(California Coast)

Achumauii
Alsoyewi
Cahuilla
Chumash
Costano
Hupa
Ipai
Karok
Luiseño
Maidu
Miwok
Monache
Pomo
Shasta
Tipai
Wappo
Wintum
Yana
Yokut
Yurok

Subarctic
(Canada and Alaska below the Arctic Circle)

Anishinabe
  (Chippewa/Northern Ojibwa)
Beaver
Carrier
Chilcotin
Chipewyan
Cree
Dogrib
Han
Hare
Ingalik
Kaska
Koyukon
Kutchin
Montagnais
Naskapi
Sarcee
Sekani
Slave
Tanaina
Tutchone
Yellowknife

Plateau
(From the Cascade Range in northwestern Canada, south to the Sierra Nevada)

Cayuse
Coeur d'Alene
Flathead
Kalispel
Klamath
Kutenai
Lillooet
Modoc
Nez Perce
Nicola
Okanagan
Palouse
Sanpoil
Shuswap
Spokane
Thompson
Umatilla

Walla Walla
Wanapam
Yakima

Great Basin
(Desert region, including Nevada and parts of Utah, California, Idaho, Wyoming, and Oregon)

Bannock
Goshute
Kawaiisu
Paiute
Shoshone
Ute
Washo

Southwest
(An area that includes Arizona, New Mexico, southern Utah, parts of Texas and northern Mexico)

Apache:
  Chiricahua
  Cibecue
  Jicarilla
  Lipan
  Mescalero
  Mimbreño
  San Carlos
  Tonto
  White Mountain
Coahuiltec
Cocopa
Havasupai
Jumeño
Karenkawa
Maricopa
Mayo
Mojave
Navajo
Pima
Pueblo:
  Hopi
  Keres
  Tano
  Tewa

Northern Tiwa
Southern Tiwa
Towa
Zuni
Quechan
Seri
Tarahumara
Tehueco
Tepecano
Tepehuan
Tohono O'odham
  (Papago)
Walapai
Yaqui
Yavapai

Plains
(Canada to southern Texas; Mississippi River, west to the Rocky Mountains)

Arapaho
Arikara
Assiniboine
Blackfoot:
  Blood
  Gros Ventre
  Piegan
  Sarcee
  Sikiska (Northern Blackfoot)
Cheyenne
Comanche
Crow
Hidatsa
Iowa
Kansa
Kiowa
Kiowa-Apache
Mandan
Missouri
Omaha
Osage
Oto
Pawnee
Ponca
Quapaw
Lakota (Sioux):

Santee
Teton
Yankton
Yanktonai
Tonkawa
Wichita

Northeast Woodlands
(Nova Scotia and
Maine, west to
Minnesota, south to
Kentucky)

Abnaki
Algonquin
Anishinabe
  (Chippewa/Ojibwa)
Beothuk
Delaware (Lenape):
  Munsee
  Unalachtigo
  Unami
Erie
Fox (Mesquakie)
Huron
Illinois
Iroquois:
  Cayuga
  Mohawk
  Onondaga
  Oneida
  Seneca
  Tuscarora
Kickapoo
Mahican
Maliseet
Massachuset
Menominee
Miami
Micmac
Mohegan
Nanticoke
Narraganset
Neutral
Ottawa
Pequot
Potawatomi
Powhatan
Sauk

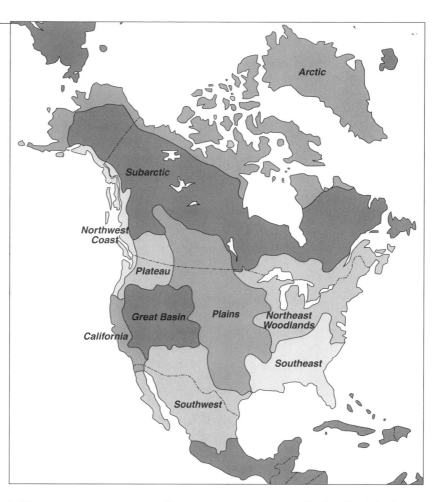

Shawnee
Susquehanna
Wampanoag
Winnebago

Southeast
(Carolinas to southern
Florida; west to Texas)

Ais
Alabama
Apalachee
Atakapa
Caddo
Calusa
Catawba
Cherokee
Chickasaw
Chitimacha

Choctaw
Coushatta
Creek
Hitchiti
Lumbee
Natchez
Seminole
Timucua
Tunica
Yamasee
Yazoo
Yuchi

Arctic
(Arctic Circle Area)

Aivilik Inuit
Aleut
Baffinland Inuit

Bering Strait Inuit
Caribou Inuit
Copper Inuit
East Greenland Inuit
Iglulik Inuit
Labrador Inuit
Mackenzie Inuit
Netsilik Inuit
North Alaskan Inuit
Pacific Yuit
Polar Inuit
Southwest Alaskan
Inuit
West Greenland Inuit

■ *From page 7–*
Many Native American dances and ceremonies, such as the Sun Dance, are never photographed because of their sacredness. Yaqui ceremonies, which unite tribal ceremonies with the Christian calendar, are an exception. The Yaqui Deer Dance symbolizes the tribe's sacred relationship to the deer spirit, which traditionally provided food, deerhide, and other necessities to the Yaqui people.

The Lakota Sun Dance is only one of many similar rituals performed by peoples of the Great Plains, the vast grassland region of central North America, and only one of hundreds of religious ceremonies that native peoples conduct throughout North America. For seventy-five years at the end of the nineteenth century and the beginning of the twentieth, it was illegal for Native Americans in the United States and Canada to observe their religious ceremonies. The survival of the Sun Dance ceremony and of many other ceremonies shows the determination of Native Americans to preserve and practice their religions, even in the face of opposition.

The History of Native American Religions

Long before European explorers reached North American shores, the land was home to hundreds of groups of Native Americans. These native peoples lived in villages that dotted the North American continent, sustaining themselves by hunting, fishing, and farming. It has been estimated that in the 1600s, before contact with European cultures, well over one million Native Americans were living in North America north of what is now the Mexican border, the area covered in this book.

Each tribe was distinct and different from the others. For one thing, each spoke its own language. Although some neighboring tribes might have languages similar enough that people could understand each other, that was not always the case. Native Americans spoke languages as different from one another as, for example, English and Hungarian. Scholars estimate that at one time there may have been 2,200 different Native American languages, and they have identified seven different language families among the Indians of the Plains alone. In that area, where tribes with very different languages often met, they developed a sign language, a kind of international code that enabled them to communicate. In addition to speaking different languages, each tribe had its own culture and customs and its own way of building homes and making clothing and everyday objects, such as tools, weapons, and utensils.

Each tribe also had its own set of beliefs and religious practices closely associated with its particular culture. There is no single "Native American religion." Similarities can be found among native religions, just as similarities can be found between Christianity and Islam or between Taoism and Buddhism, but the religious customs of different tribes can be and are quite varied.

Comparisons to Other Religions

Native American religions differ from "organized" religions in several ways. They are not "systematic." In other words, they have no church buildings and no church hierarchy, or organizational structure. Although some tribal tales recall the deeds of famous tribe members, most Native American religions do not rely on a central historical figure or figures, such as Moses, Jesus, Allah, or Buddha, and they are not tied to specific historical events, such as Christ's crucifixion or Buddha's enlightenment.

Traditional Native American culture has always been oral, with information passed down by word of mouth. There is no written set of beliefs, no code of ethics, no "rules" that "followers" must adhere to. There is no holy book, such as the Bible or Koran. In many ways, Native American spirituality is similar to other religions with folk roots, such as Shinto or Taoism. The fact that there is no written creed does not suggest that there were no standards of behavior or ethics, however. Strict rules for living a decent and ethical life governed all Native American cultures. Tribe members were taught by example, and those guiding principles were not memorized in formal lessons but were internalized from childhood and became a part of their lives.

When European settlers first came into contact with Native peoples, the differences they saw led them to conclude that the Indians had no religion, or at least no "real" religion. The Native Americans they met had no written language so there were no books from which the newcomers might learn about native religions. In addition, few non-Indians bothered to learn Native American languages, and the Native Americans often deliberately excluded the outsiders from their holiest rituals. Not until the early years of the twentieth century did people finally begin to examine Native American belief systems. They found that far from being simple "nature worship," Native American beliefs were often rich, deep, and complex.

■ *Eagle Feathers*

Flying higher than any other bird, the eagle embodies a strong spiritual presence, one that communicates between earth and the most powerful forces of the universe. Eagle feathers are used ritually by many tribes to invoke the bird's spirit power.

In recent years, as knowledge of Native American customs has become more widespread, so has respect for their religious traditions. Many Native Americans have returned to their roots, seeking spiritual renewal in traditional rituals and practices. Ceremonies for purification and healing, for celebrating the cycles of nature, and for renewing the land attract participants and observers from many backgrounds, those people who find the ceremonies and celebrations spiritually meaningful.

Basic Concepts

Although the ways of expressing spiritual belief vary widely from region to region and tribe to tribe, certain basic concepts or ideas do occur in most Native American religions.

- A Great Power, sometimes called Great Spirit or Great Mystery (*Wakan Tanka, Manitou, Orenda*, among other names) underlies all creation. This power is not a personal god, such as the Judeo-Christian God, and it cannot be imagined in human form. Rather, it is a universal force to which all of nature is attuned. All of nature, including human nature, is the creation of this Great Power.

- All things in the universe are alive and contain spirit within them. Spirit forces actively affect human lives in ways that can be both good and bad. The earth, which nourishes and sustains life, and to which people return after death, is particularly endowed with spirit and is to be respected and revered. All forms of life depend on all others.

- The individual is called on to "walk in the sacred way"—that is, to live in balance and harmony with the universe and the spirit world. People find their own sacred way by seeking clues to the sacred in dreams and visions.

- Values, beliefs, morals, ethics, and sacred traditions are passed on through an oral tradition and through ceremonies. Cultural bonding takes place through rituals developed by each group over centuries. These commonly include dancing, singing, drumming, and feasting, as well as purification rites, fasting, and physical ordeals.

- Certain people (sometimes called shamans, medicine men or women, or singers) have special ties to the higher powers. Their special calling enables them to mediate between the spirit world and the earthly world for healing, spiritual renewal, and the good of the community.
- Humor is a part of the sacred way because people need to be reminded of their foolishness.

Origins of Native American Religions

Native American religions go back to distant prehistory. Scholars who study ancient cultures believe that the ancestors of the Native Americans may have migrated to the North American continent from Asia more than twelve thousand or more years ago, traveling across a land bridge that once linked Siberia to Alaska across what is now the Bering Strait. These peoples moved in bands, or tribes, gradually spreading south and east across North America. These first Americans probably brought their religious beliefs with them, gradually adapting them to the land they settled.

In Native American religions, students of prehistory find a continuous thread of shamanism, humankind's "oldest religion," in which mediation between the visible and spirit worlds is brought about by shamans. Shamans, or holy people, are healers and interpreters of the will of the spirit world, and shamanism is one of the earliest traceable forms of religion. Another feature of shamanism was animism, the belief that all things contain spirit, or life. This was a distinctive feature of Native American religion.

Scholars point to religious similarities between the Siberian tribes of Asia and the Inuit tribes of Canada and Alaska. The parallels they find suggest that these religions have common origins. Native American religions also share ideas—particularly about the importance of balance and harmony with the universe—with Asian religions such as Taoism and Confucianism, which developed in ancient China out of the same religious roots, and with Shinto, the native religion of Japan, which had the same Asian influences.

The traditions of native peoples themselves, however, often hold that their tribes originated in their ancestral lands and spread outward from there. The Navajo, for example, point to a place in the mountains of southeastern Colorado where the First People emerged from the underworld and began to create life on this earth. Similarly, the Umatilla of eastern Washington State hold that their people were created in that place and have been there since the beginning of time. The creation stories of most Native Americans support their beliefs that they have always been in North America, connected to and part of the land.

Native Americans Today

Approximately two and a half million people living in the United States and Canada identify themselves as Native Americans. What makes someone a Native American is a matter of both heritage and law. Some tribal groups, such as the Cherokee, admit to full tribal membership anyone who can trace any Cherokee ancestry; other tribes admit only those who are at least one-quarter or one-eighth Native American by blood; still other tribes have other rules governing tribal membership.

The native peoples who live on tribal lands, such as the Hopi and the Navajo in the southwestern United States and the Inuit peoples in Alaska and Canada, are most likely to have preserved the religious practices of their forebears and continued their religious traditions. Most people who declare themselves to be Native American, however, whether they live on reservations or in cities, do follow at least some Native American cultural and religious practices and attempt to pass on their culture and sacred history to the next generation.

One Sacred Way

Native Americans do not segment their lives into the secular and the religious. Their culture and their religion are one, so closely united that many Native American languages have no word for "religion." All work is considered prayer. A woman making a basket may pray to the spirit of the grass as she cuts it. Later, the designs she weaves into the basket may have symbolic meaning. The art of basketry itself is a kind of spiritual gift for which to be grateful. The successfully completed basket, too, a work of both beauty and usefulness, is an occasion for thanks. Thus even a common utensil has a sacred dimension. Hunters and farmers invoke the spirits of game and fertility so that their efforts and the outcome of their labors will be blessed. Ideally, people live with a constant awareness of the spirit world around them and act in ways that honor this awareness.

Although they do not separate their religion from their everyday existence, Native Americans have traditionally believed in a higher power that created and informs all of life, and they have followed traditions and rituals meant to connect humans with that power, the basic tenet of all religions. Whether their traditions came with them from another continent or sprang from American soil, the religions of native peoples represent an ancient tradition of deep spirituality.

■ *Powwows, gatherings that cut across tribal lines, encourage today's Native Americans to participate in traditional dances and cultural exchanges.*

CHAPTER **2**

The Spirit World and the Sacred Way

*T*he Algonquins speak of *Manitou*, the Iroquois of *Orenda*, the Lakota of *Wakan Tanka*, words usually translated as "Great Spirit" or "Great Mystery." These words all refer to the indefinable "Power" that underlies all creation. However else their traditions may vary, almost all Native American peoples believe in a great sacred force from which all things come and which keeps the universe in motion.

The Great Spirit

When native peoples first came in contact with European religions, they recognized parallels between the white man's God and their Great Spirit, and some groups incorporated the notion of a personal god into their beliefs. But traditionally, the Great Spirit is not a supreme being, such as the Judeo-Christian God or Islam's Allah, who speaks to humankind. It is more like the Tao of Taoism, an immense and universal power that is above and in all things. The words *Wakan Tanka*, for example, literally mean "most sacred," and when people speak of Wakan Tanka, they are more likely to be speaking of the sacred power of the universe rather than of a personal god.

■ Preceeding page–
Spider Rock (right) and
Speaking Rock (left) in
Canyon de Chelly
National Monument are
sacred sites. Spider
Rock is the traditional
home of Spider Woman,
a legendary holy person
who taught the Navajo
the art of weaving.

> ### ■ Wakan Power
>
> *The most wonderful things which a man can do are different from the works of nature. When the seasons changed, we regarded it as a gift from the sun, which is the strongest of all the mysterious wakan powers....We cannot see the thunder, and we say it is wakan, but we see the lightning and we know that the thunder and the lightning are a sign of rain, which does good to the earth. Anything which has a similar power is wakan, but above all is the sun, which has the most power of all...*
>
> —Anonymous, Teton Sioux
>
> from *Teton Sioux Music,* by Francis Densmore, 1918. Reprinted in *The Sacred: Ways of Knowledge, Sources of Life,* by Peggy V. Beck, Anna Lee Walters, and Nia Francisco. Tasile, Ariz.: Navajo Community College Press, 1977, 1992.

The Great Spirit cannot be seen or touched, but it is present in the cycles and visible signs of nature. People can find evidence of it in the continuing change of seasons; in day and night; growth and death; and in the movement of the sun, moon, and stars.

People traditionally learned about the Great Spirit, or Great Mystery, through oral tradition, the tales of magical beings and important events and ancestors, passed down from one generation to the next. They also experience this mysterious power directly, through dreams and visions. Children learn from an early age to pay attention to their dreams and to examine them for meaning. They learn to be aware of the spirit world, which is all around them, a kind of parallel universe that is always close at hand. Later in life, they may actively seek a vision for spiritual guidance through periods of fasting and self-denial.

The Creator

Although all things come from the Great Spirit, the Great Spirit is not the creator of the world. In Native American belief, that function is performed by a supernatural being with special creative powers, a being whom scholars call a culture hero. This being may have human form, such as First Man and First Woman of the Navajo, World-Maker of the Yakima, or Earth

Starter of the Ojibwa, or a dual human/animal form, such as Raven of the Northwest or Coyote of the western Plains. In addition to creating the world and placing humans on it, he or she gives the first human beings the ceremonies and cultural institutions that they will use on earth.

The World of Spirits

A central concept of Native American religions is the idea that everything in the world that can be seen or touched is "alive" with spirit, or breath. All of the environment has a life. The water that comes out of the earth is alive, as are the rocks and the hills. Each comes from the earth, which is itself alive and revered as the mother—or, as some say, grandmother—of all. The spirit of the air can be felt in a breath of wind and the sound of the breeze as it moves through the leaves. The spirit of the rain can be felt in moisture on the earth. The spirits of rocks, trees, grass, wind, and rain cannot be seen, but they are a constant reality, influencing all aspects of human life.

Several different kinds of spirits inhabit the world.

- The sky beings, such as star gods, the sun, and the moon
- Spirits of the atmosphere, such as the four winds, whirlwinds, rain, and Thunderbird, a huge bird—perhaps like an eagle—whose flapping wings create thunder and whose flashing eyes create lightning
- The rulers of animals and plants, such as Buffalo Spirit or Corn Spirit; also those connected with natural places such as mountains, waterfalls, and the sea
- The powers of the underworld, such as Mother or Grandmother Earth, snakes and cougars, and the ruler of the dead

The spirits of the dead may live as ghosts on earth or may be reborn as animals. Ghosts are potentially dangerous, however, and are to be avoided for the harm they can do.

Sky Spirits

Many people shared the belief that the Milky Way, the broad band of faint light that can be seen in the night sky, was a

■ **Teton Sioux Prayer**
Wakan Tanka
when I pray to him
heard me
whatever is good
he grants me

  —sung by Lone Man

from *American Indian Literature, an Anthology.* Alan R. Velie, editor. Tucson, Ariz: University of Arizona Press, 1979.

"path of souls" to which people went after death. The Luiseño of California explain that the First People went to the sky when their work on earth was done, taking their families with them and becoming star people. The Navajo think of stars as "friend-ly beings" because they lighten the night sky and also because the stars help them tell time and mark the seasons.

According to Pawnee creation stories, their tribe is descend-ed from the Morning Star. In their tales, Morning Star overcame the others and directed them to stand in their appointed places. Morning Star wed Evening Star, and their daughter traveled to earth, where she married the child of the sun and the moon. From this union came the Pawnee people.

■ *The bear spirit, one of the strongest and wisest of the animal spirits, is considered a powerful healing force by Pueblo, Lakota, and Anishinabe (Chippewa) peoples. This modern bear carv-ing is the work of artist Russell Sanchez.*

In the Southwest, the sun has special significance. The Zuni welcome the sun each day as "father," sprinkling a little corn meal and offering a prayer to this great power that awakens the earth's fertility. And in California, the Chumash hold the sun to be the greatest supernatural being, the one who carries the torch that lights the world. He is both loved and feared, because although he brings light and heat, he also brings death.

Animal Spirits

In their mythic histories, many tribes recall a time when there was no distinction between animals and humans. All spoke the same language, and each received special powers from the creator who made them. Humans, indeed, are often portrayed as the weakest and least able of all the beings in creation. Animals such as bear and badger, deer and mice are seen as having distinct spirits and, indeed, as being "people" of another order.

Many spirit beings, such as Raven of the Tlingit and Buffalo Calf Woman who brought the Lakota their seven sacred rites, have the ability to change from animal to human and back again. Animal spirits may convey the traits attributed to that animal, such as speed or courage. Birds, especially the eagle, are respected for their freedom in flight. The oral traditions of many tribes portray birds as special beings with the power to carry messages to the sky and back to earth. For this reason, the feathers of the eagle are a mark of special power and esteem.

Native hunters traditionally prayed to the spirit of the game they killed for food, thanking the deer, the buffalo, or the salmon for giving up its life so that people might eat and remain alive. People understood that only with the help of the spirit world could they succeed in life. Someone who neglected to respect the life of the deer he had taken might find that the other deer spirits rose up against him and hindered future hunts. In Cherokee tradition, certain illnesses, such as rheumatism or arthritis, came to the hunter who ignored his duty to honor the animals he hunted.

Plant Spirits

Plants also have spirit, which can be seen in the way they respond to their environment. Plants that are not cared for and treated with respect do not survive. If they are over-harvested, they will not return. They draw their spirit from the earth, as do other living things. Native Americans saw plants as friendly to humans. To native peoples there were few, if any, plants that could not be used as food, as medicine, in making shelter or useful objects, or in rituals. Many different tribes viewed certain food plants, particularly maize (Indian corn), beans, and squash or pumpkin, as gifts of divine origin, provided by the Great Spirit for their use. These traditional foods, grown and eaten by the many agricultural tribes that lived on a largely vegetarian diet, provided balanced nutrition that kept people healthy and strong.

Native people lived particularly close to the land and had a deep understanding of its value. Everything was not sacred, but almost anything, particularly if it was used to help sustain life, might be sacred, and its spirit had to be respected. People had to act in ways that would keep the world in balance and harmony. Overusing a plant or killing too much game could result in total loss. But recognizing the spiritual dimension of all things kept native hunters and gatherers constantly aware of their responsibility to save and preserve them even as they used them to preserve their own lives.

Sacred Tobacco

Native Americans considered tobacco a sacred plant and used it in rituals as a way of communicating with the spirit world. They grew and cured a special, strong tobacco. Its scented smoke, rising to the skies, carried human prayers to the spirits. Among the Crow, just planting and growing tobacco brought good fortune, and they performed rituals for its planting and harvest. Tobacco was widely grown, and tribes that did not grow it traded for it with other tribes. Present-day rituals still make use of tobacco.

As part of a ceremony, holy men and tribal leaders smoked tobacco in a pipe or rolled into a cigar, or they sprinkled it on an open fire. They also placed dried tobacco leaves on waters or on the ground as an offering. Many tribes had tales concerning its sacredness, in which it was described as a special gift from the spirit world.

The Spirit in Places

Places were particularly endowed with spiritual significance. Mountain spirits, water spirits, lake spirits, rock spirits—all interacted to make a particular area sacred. Within their tribal boundaries, groups had areas—high mountains, bluffs, dense woods, springs, lakes and waterfalls—that had special spiritual power, much as a great cathedral or a temple might have for a Christian or a Buddhist. People went to these places to seek

■ *Here is a medicine wheel at Bighorn Mountains, Wyoming, a sacred site for Native Americans.*

■ **Medicine Wheels**

The ancestors of the Plains Indians left behind hundreds of stone circles, often laid out like the spokes of a wheel around a central cairn, or pile of rocks, and with other cairns placed at intervals around them. Archaeologists now believe that these medicine wheels, as they are called, helped Native Americans follow the progress of the year by charting the movement of the sun and stars. Medicine wheels are associated with spirit forces, and the land on which they lie is sacred. Sacrifices and sacred items were often left within them.

The Bighorn Medicine Wheel lies atop a mountain in Wyoming's Bighorn National Forest. It is sacred to several Plains tribes and has been in continuous use as a religious site for centuries. More than eighty feet in diameter, this medicine wheel has twenty-eight spokes that extend from the central cairn to the edge.

communion with the Great Spirit, to conduct ceremonies and rituals, and to be healed. In the Navajo tradition, for example, there are four kinds of sacred land:

- Lands mentioned in sacred stories
- Lands where supernatural events occurred
- Lands where healing plants, minerals, or waters can be found
- Lands where people can communicate with spirits

Land might become sacred when people experienced visions there or, in some cultures, when tribe members were buried on it. Creation stories and other parts of the oral tradition were often tied to specific places, giving the tribe's ancestral grounds special spiritual meaning.

Interaction with the Spirit World

In Native American belief, people interact continually with spirits, both seen and unseen, as they interact with the natural world. The spirit world speaks to those who are attuned to it. The spirits require respect and attention. If no one speaks to them, they may in turn refuse to speak. Spirits may desert a place that is abused or neglected or allowed to become polluted. Those who have the gift of understanding the spirit world see the loss of spirit in the disappearance of plant and animal life or in crop failure, drought, and misfortune. If the spirit world is not respected, the earth itself might die, and all that is on it will die as well. People therefore have a responsibility to maintain life on earth by praying continually to its spirits and by walking in the sacred way, in harmony with nature.

Sacred Objects

Almost all groups of Native Americans had a tradition of the "medicine bundle," a collection of objects with sacred significance and spirit power, wrapped in an animal skin or in cloth. A medicine bundle might belong to an individual or a family, or it might be the sacred object of a tribe or clan.

Medicine bundles are considered to be alive and are treated with great respect. To be entrusted with the care of a medicine bundle is both a great honor and a grave responsibility. Proper care of the medicine bundle may carry with it the power to cure, assure good hunting, or give the caretaker the ability to foresee the future. Mistreating or failing to respect the bundle with its sacred objects can bring disaster.

Among the Navajo, the contents of the medicine bundle depend on what ritual a singer, or spiritual leader, performs. All the items are in some way connected to the particular part of the creation story that will be sung in the ceremony. They might include natural items, such as shells, stones, crystals, and feathers; sacred representations of spirit gods, such as carvings; and other tools of the singer's calling.

■ *The masks and headdresses worn by these White Mountain Apache dancers transform them into gan, the mountain spirits of the Apache, who bring good fortune and communicate with the higher powers of the universe.*

Besides the medicine bundle, tribes may have other objects of special spiritual significance. The sacred pipe of the Lakota, a gift to the Lakota people from Buffalo Calf Woman, the spirit messenger from the Buffalo People, is one such item. The Pueblo peoples of the Southwest prepare *paho,* sacred prayer sticks that are carved and decorated with stones, shells, and, especially, feathers, which help to convey the breath of the prayer to the spirits. After making the prayer sticks, people place them where spirits are likely to find them and honor the prayers they carry. They are usually used as petitions for rain or good health and, by the Zuni, after a family death.

Masks are another kind of sacred object. They are considered to have spirit life within them; masks worn in sacred dances are believed to have the power to transform the dancer into the being portrayed by the mask. Masks are cared for with respect and honored with regular feasts.

Cultures for whom masks have special sacred meaning include the Huron of the Northeast, the tribes of the Northwest Coast, and the Hopi of the Southwest, whose colorful *kachinas,* fanciful carved figures that incorporate symbols of the earth and sky, the atmosphere, and the plant and animal kingdoms, represent the spirit world.

Shamans

All Native American groups traditionally have spiritual leaders, members of the community who have special connections to the spirit world. These people are often called shamans, or medicine people. The word *shaman* comes from a similar word used by Siberian tribes to describe their holy people. *Shaman* is now widely used to describe the spiritual leaders of Native American groups, but the names used by the shamans themselves are more descriptive: dream doctor; dreamer; singer; clairvoyant, or one able to see the future clearly; shadow man; head full of songs. The Penobscot call their shaman drum-sound man because of the drumming he does as part of the ritual to call helping spirits.

The term *medicine man* (or *medicine woman*), used to describe a shaman, is a European label. French explorers described native healers with the French word *médecin*, meaning "doctor." Native peoples later extended the meaning of *medicine* to mean "spiritual power," because according to their understanding, the individuals the French called medicine men were those who were in touch with the higher powers of the universe and could bring them to bear on a problem.

In some cultures, particularly in the far North, the shaman or medicine person is one who can enlist the help of the spirits by leaving his body and traveling to the spirit world, which can be a dark and dangerous place. In general, spirit power is neutral, but it can be used either for good or for evil, and controlling it is a difficult and exacting task.

As a rule, young women cannot be shamans because of the power of their fertility, but in a number of cultures, women may become shamans, as opposed to herbalists or healers of common illnesses, when they pass childbearing age. The shamans of several tribes of northern California, such as the Hupa, Shasta, and Chilula, are usually women. Among other California tribes, both men and women may be shamans. The Lakota of the western Plains call a medicine woman *wapiye' win,* or "spirit-calling woman," one who receives information from the spirit world.

Shamans might be called on to cure illness, to find lost objects, to influence the weather, or to predict the likely outcome of a course of action. Therefore, a shaman develops many skills and abilities, such as seeing into the future, interpreting dreams, storytelling and acting as tribal historian, finding lost objects, knowing the uses of herbs and plants, and diagnosing ailments. Shamans often specialize in different aspects of spiritual life. Some are primarily prophets, seers, or visionaries who foresee the future. Others are healers. Others may be holy men who perform public ceremonies or lead rituals for the tribe as a whole.

Becoming a Shaman

People might become shamans in a variety of ways, depending on their culture. In some tribes, shamans are those people who are visited spontaneously by spirits, often from childhood or during an episode of illness. In other groups, shamanistic secrets are inherited, passed down to those family members who are willing and able to take on the vocation. And finally, people who wish to become shamans and feel they have the necessary gifts may undertake study with other shamans. Apache shamans, for example, reach their position mainly through study. They must master a great deal of information that is passed down orally and learn to conduct the sacred ceremonies of their tribe, a process that includes receiving details of how to perform rituals through dreams and visions. But even if becoming a shaman is a matter of choice, there is an element of "calling." If the spirits do not speak to an individual, he or she cannot become a shaman. The ability to receive visions, either to foretell the future or to diagnose illnesses, is a necessary part of being a shaman, and the most powerful shamans are those

■ Shamans use spirit helpers, or guardian spirits, to communicate with the spirit world. A guardian spirit often took the form of an animal.

people who are called by spirits to serve their tribe, even some-times against their will.

Among the Inuit, someone who is called to be a shaman leaves society and works with a master. The shaman-to-be undergoes a symbolic death and resurrection, during which time he acquires one or more guardian spirits, or spirit helpers, that will assist him in contacting the higher powers. He learns to travel by means of visions to the spirit worlds, either under the sea or above the sky, in order to help others. For instance, if hunting was going badly, an Inuit shaman might travel to the spirit world to find out why.

Among the Ojibwa of Canada and the northern United States, many members of the tribe might belong to a medicine society—that is, they are initiated into the most basic secrets of tribal ritual. Such secrets might include using the drum to expel harmful spirits, magical songs and chants, and the powers of herbal medicines, along with ritual patterns and beliefs. Within the society are different levels of mastery; at the top are the shamans, who have mastered the skills and self-discipline necessary to fulfill the position's responsibilities.

Guardian Spirits

Shamans use spirit helpers, or guardian spirits, to communicate with the spirit world. Although in some tribes anyone may seek and have a guardian spirit, a shaman commonly has more than one, perhaps six or more, each of which may have different powers. The shaman contacts and draws on the aid of these helpers by falling into a trance. Some shamans are able to reach the trance state spontaneously, at will. Others prepare themselves for contact with the spirit world by fasting, withdrawing to solitude, self-denial, drumming, or such physical exertions as dancing.

The tradition of having a personal guardian spirit that connected an individual to the spirit world was widespread among Native Americans in almost every part of North America. In southwestern groups such as the Pueblo, the guardian spirit came to the infant at birth and stayed with him or her throughout life. In cultures where successful hunting was necessary to sustain life, boys or young men often went in search of a guardian spirit to help them as they assumed the responsibilities of adulthood.

To acquire a guardian spirit, the spirit-seeker went on a vision quest. Isolation in a sacred place, fasting, and prayer were the basic elements of such a quest. Among the Ojibwa, when a boy reached maturity, tribal elders took him to a solitary place where they had made a platform in a pine tree. There the boy waited, fasting, until a vision came to him. If the spirits willed it, he received a vision with information about how he might live a worthy life. At that time, a guardian spirit might appear to him to guide and protect him.

A guardian spirit usually took the form of an animal, but in some cases the form might be that of a natural element, such as wind or fire. The spirit the boy saw brought him special powers; for example, a turtle spirit might confer long life; an eagle spirit, purity and fierceness; a butterfly spirit, the ability to escape danger; or a bear spirit, strength. Among the Plains tribes, buffalo spirits were especially powerful; the buffalo, whose flesh gave food, whose bones became tools, and whose hide made clothing and shelter, was considered a special messenger of the Great Spirit.

■ In Native American religions, eagles are considered sacred because of their special powers–the ability to carry messages between sky and earth.

Where it was tradition for individuals, rather than families or the whole tribe, to have a medicine bundle, the spirit might instruct the spirit-seeker in making one. Taboos, the actions that the seeker would need to avoid in order to live a good and healthy life, often came to someone in the vision, along with a sacred song, chant, or dance. New names were often bestowed at that time. Individuals who received guardian spirits could then call on them for help throughout their lives.

In some traditions, particularly in the Plateau region of the Northwest, every boy in the tribe sought a guardian spirit, and men might seek a vision for spiritual guidance throughout their lives. Some groups permitted young girls to go on vision quests as well. Others, as widely scattered as the Algonquin in the Northeast and the Inuit of Alaska and Canada, expected only those who wished to become holy people to acquire guardian spirits, which would help them in healing and other ceremonies.

Living with the Spirit World

The Native American way has always been to respect and honor the spirits of all natural things. All things on earth are alive and more or less equal—in fact, people are in many ways the weakest and least well equipped of earth's creatures, dependent on the bounty of the earth for their lives. Angering or neglecting the spirits of the animals, plants, and other forms of the living earth might cause illness for an individual or disaster for the entire community. Listening to the spirits and treating them with respect is therefore an essential part of everyday life.

Traditionally, Native Americans pray with gladness to the spirit of the sun for each new day, they praise the food that the earth has grown for them, they pray as they go about their work and as they experience nature around them. "The Native way," says Corbin Harney, a spiritual leader of the Shoshone Nation, "is to pray for everything."

CHAPTER 3

Creating the World:
The Oral Tradition

n long winter evenings, Native Americans often gathered around a fire and told tales of times long ago, when the world was new and humans and animals spoke the same language. Although the stories might have been amusing, storytelling was far more than simple entertainment. It was the principal means by which cultural values and beliefs were passed from one generation to the next. The time between the harvest festival in early fall and the renewal festival of early spring, the coldest and darkest time of the year, was an important period in Native American life. It was the time when all members of the tribe, both young and old, came together to be reminded of their shared past and culture.

Native American religions do not have a sacred book on which people rely for spiritual guidance. Their sacred lore is traditionally passed down orally, in stories of how the world was made, how the people came to be, and how they received the customs that make up their culture. The tales that make up a tribe's sacred tradition are told and retold throughout a person's lifetime, so that each man, woman, and child carries within himself or herself a knowledge of the tribe's culture and belief.

Native American stories of creation and the actions of heroes and spirits are sacred to them in much the same way that the Bible is sacred to Christians and Jews; the Koran, to Muslims; and the sutras, scriptural narratives that are often regarded as discourses of the Buddha, to Buddhists.

In general, the tales in Native American oral tradition are organized in cycles rather than in a linear fashion. Even when the tales are written down, they do not form a step-by-step narrative like that in the Judeo-Christian Bible, which is largely an account of the wanderings of the Jewish people and the events connected with the life of Jesus and the early Christian Church. Instead, Native American stories usually cluster around three time periods: early creation, when all beings spoke the same language and could understand each other; the era of the culture hero, a divine being who prepared the world for humankind and taught people their sacred customs; and finally, present time, in which people now live and try to follow the will of the spirits.

Native American tales often place the tribe in the center of the universe, explaining how they came to be in a particular place. For each tribe, this god-given land was sacred. It fed them with crops and game, supplied them with clothes and shelter, and they returned to it after death, becoming part of the cycle of life. Each tribe also had sacred places within its territory, where visions or encounters with the spirit world might occur and where sacred rituals were held.

The Beginnings of the World

Native American tales usually assume that the universe is timeless and that some kind of universe has always existed. Often in those tales, the world is covered with water, which must give way to dry land so that humans can live there.

Into this unformed world, either from the heavens above or by emerging from deep within the earth, powerful supernatural forces, usually in the form of a divine being, come to change the existing universe into the world as we now know it. The supernatural beings who create the world are not the same as the Great Spirit. They are often not even the first beings in the universe. They are culture heroes, beings of divine origins and mythic proportions who came to the people in the distant past to prepare the land for them and teach them the traditions and customs they must follow.

Sky Woman of the Iroquois

In the Northeast woodlands, which extended from what is now Nova Scotia, Canada, to the Great Lakes region, the Iroquois and neighboring tribes traced their origins to a holy being called Sky Woman, who fell through a torn place in the sky. The story of Sky Woman illustrates how a Native American tale weaves together a number of threads that help to explain life and belief. It tells how the earth was formed; presents the sacred origins for the foods on which the people relied for their lives and health—squash, beans, and corn; offers a rationale for why good and evil must coexist in the world; and gives an explanation for why people must eventually die.

According to one version of the tale, the huge sea that covered the world already contained sea birds, turtles, and other water creatures when Sky Woman came tumbling out of the heavens. Two loons flew beneath her and caught her and called the other animals to help. A turtle appeared and took the woman on his broad back. The animals discussed what to do. Finally, they decided that the Sky Woman needed earth. One by one, they dived to the bottom of the sea to try to get soil. The beaver failed to come up with anything, and so did the muskrat. Finally, the toad came up with a little dirt in his mouth. The woman took the dirt and put it on the turtle's back. The small patch of earth grew and grew and formed the earth, which still rests on the turtle's back.

After the earth was formed, Sky Woman gave birth to twin sons. They, too, were supernatural beings whose job it was to prepare the earth for humans. In giving birth to the second twin, Sky Woman died. She was buried, but her gifts to the Iroquoian people did not end. From her body came the plants that nourish them—the pumpkin (squash) from her head, corn from her body, and beans from her legs.

Sky Woman's Twins

Sky Woman's twins were the creators of the world as humans know it. The first-born twin, Tijus-keha, called Master of Life by the

Iroquois, was good. He watched over humans, created animals and plants, and gave people customs to follow. The other twin, Tawis-karong, was evil. He made animals that preyed on humans—wolves, bears, and snakes. To irritate humankind, he made giant mosquitoes. He also made a huge toad that drank up all the water on earth so humans would die of thirst.

Tijus-keha could not completely undo his brother's deeds, but he could lessen their effects. He sent the dove and the partridge to find water. The partridge found all of Tawis-karong's monstrous creations waiting to take over the earth. When the partridge returned and reported what she had seen, Tijus-keha went to his brother's land. He cut open the giant toad and returned water to humans. Then he reduced the size of all his brother's creatures, including the toad and the mosquito, so the harm they could do humans would be slight.

Sky Woman appeared to Tijus-keha in a dream and told him that he must challenge his brother for the right to rule the world. The two met in a fight to the death. At last, Tijus-keha

---

■ *The Zuni Emerge*

These lines from the Zuni emergence tale tell how the first Zuni people passed through different worlds on their journey to earth. The "precious things" they carried were the fetishes, or small sacred images, that bring rain and crops.

Our great fathers talked together. Here they arose and moved on. They stooped over and came out from the fourth world, carrying their precious things clasped to their breasts.

They stooped over and came out from moss world, carrying their precious things clasped to their breasts.
They stooped over and came out from mud world, carrying their precious things clasped to their breasts.
They stooped over and came out from wing world, carrying their precious things clasped to their breasts.
They stooped over and came out and saw their Sun Father and inhaled the sacred breath of the light of day.

from *The Zuni* by M.C. Stevenson, trans. In "The Zuni Indians," Bureau of American Ethnology, 23rd. Annual Report, 1901–02. Reprinted in *In the Trail of the Wind*, John Bierhorst, ed., 1971.

won. But his brother did not die completely. Tawis-karong told Tijus-keha that in the end, he would win, for all people would eventually follow him to the west, the land of death.

The First People and Changing Woman of the Navajo

In the oral tradition of Native American peoples, stories were not memorized word for word, but told and retold so that their message became part of each speaker and listener. Thus details of creation stories vary widely, not only from area to area and tribe to tribe but even within tribes. A creation story is not a single tale, or even a collection of stories. It is more like a tree with many branches spreading out in all directions but eventually going back to the same trunk. The same stories may be told in many different ways, but the basic ideas that underlie the stories remain constant.

Several southwestern groups tell emergence tales—stories in which the first people on earth were not created but emerged from the last of a series of underworlds. The Navajo tell how First Man and First Woman and other *Diyin Diné,* or "Holy People," had to come up through a succession of underworlds where other beings lived. In the lower worlds, the people fought and behaved badly, causing disorder and confusion. The strife brought on by their bad actions destroyed the world, and they had to move on.

As they traveled from world to world, the Diné realized that they needed to learn to live in harmony and order. Finally, they emerged onto the last layer of the earth, which was formless and covered with water. Talking God spoke to them and told them how to drain the water and make dry land.

Talking God told First Man how to build a shelter. On its floor, First Man laid the contents of the medicine bundle that he had carried with him through the layers of the underworld. The pattern the sacred objects made on the ground showed what the features of the world would be.

Then First Man and First Woman created the world. They fashioned the four sacred mountains of the Navajo universe. They put Blanca Peak in the east, fastened it with a bolt of white lightning, and laid a blanket of daylight over it. In the south they placed Mount Taylor, wrapped in the blue of the sky. In the west, they spread out the San Francisco Peaks, splashed with the yellow of the sun. And in the north, they put Hesperus Peak, cloaked in darkness. The Navajo associate each cardinal direction, or compass point, with its own special color and power.

First Man Finds Changing Woman

Although their culture developed thousands of miles from the lands of the Iroquoians, the Navajo tell stories with similar elements. A central figure in their tales is Changing Woman, who, like Sky Woman, is responsible for the gift of corn and who bears twin sons. Like Sky Woman, she also has divine origins.

After he and First Woman created the world, First Man went walking in the mountains. On a black and stormy night, he heard a baby cry. He went to the sound of the crying and found a baby lying in a cradle of rainbows, its head to the west and its feet to the east. It was wrapped in four blankets, blue, black, white, and yellow, held in place by a sunbeam. First Man gathered up the baby and took it home to First Woman. There they removed the blankets and saw that the baby was a girl.

Each day that passed was like a year. In four days, the girl was grown. Her parents named her White Shell Woman, but she is usually called Changing Woman.

Changing Woman gave birth to twins whose father was the sun. The twins, Monster Slayer and Born for Water, grew quickly and left to be with their father. He gave them special knowledge and powerful weapons with which they destroyed the dangerous monsters that had been threatening the Holy People.

Changing Woman used the medicine bundle that she received from First Man to create maize, the corn that is the staple of the Navajo diet. Finally, she made Earth People from flakes of her own skin and set them on the earth, and so the Navajo came to be.

To the sacred story of the creation of the world, the Navajo trace many of their customs and ceremonies. The lives of Changing Woman and her sons became models for their own lives. Navajo healing rituals seek to return the sick person to the state of harmony and balance that existed when the world was new.

Earth Starter of the Maidu

The culture hero of the Maidu Indians of the California coast is Earth Starter, who came down from the sky on a rope of feathers to a dark world covered with water. There he found Turtle and a companion, Pehe-ipe, floating on a raft. Earth Starter sent Turtle to the bottom of the waters to get earth. The distance was so great that Turtle did not return for six years. When he did, most of the earth he had scooped up had washed away. Only a little was left under his claws. But Earth Starter scraped it out and made a tiny ball. He put it on the raft, and soon it grew to be the world.

As yet, there was no light in the world. Earth Starter told Turtle and Pehe-ipe to look to the east, and the sun appeared in the form of a beautiful young woman. Earth Starter beckoned to her to come toward them, and she did, only to vanish in the west. The darkness seemed even greater, and Turtle and Pehe-ipe were frightened, so Earth Starter put the stars in the sky. Knowing that the sun would return, he created the oak so that creatures could sit in the shade. The coyote and the rattlesnake came up from underground, and Earth Starter called birds to come down from the sky. He made other animals, and he made plants. Then he made the first people—Kuksu, the first man, and Morning-Star Woman. Their children filled the world.

One day Earth Starter took the first man to a lake. He was very old, and he tumbled in and was swallowed up by the water. At last he emerged, young again. Earth Starter explained that this was how it would be with people. They would forever grow old and go down, then rise up anew. Earth Starter returned to the sky, leaving people on earth.

Trickster Tales

Nearly every Native American story cycle has tales centered on a character we call a trickster. The trickster is a supernatural being, often the brother or sister of a culture hero, who plays practical jokes on people, undoing the good works of the culture hero or otherwise making trouble. In the Iroquoian story of Sky Woman, the second twin is the trickster. Tricksters account for many of the ills and petty annoyances humans experience. Because tricksters, too, have supernatural origins, humans must put up with their pranks.

Some tricksters, such as the Iroquoian twin Tawis-karong, the Old Man of the Crow and the Blackfoot, or the Winnebago trickster Wakdjunkga, were more or less human in form. Many other tricksters were animals with human characteristics: the Shoshone and other western tribes had Coyote; the Lakota had Inktomi, or "spider"; the Ojibwa, Hare; the Seminole, Rabbit; the Luiseño, Frog Woman. Whether human or animal, they have special powers that can be used for either good or harm, but they also have great shortcomings. They behave in bawdy, irresponsible, selfish ways, breaking taboos and defying accepted standards. They often end up suffering for their actions, but they always survive to trick again. A trickster is often the butt of broad humor, someone to laugh at. Not infrequently, his tricks backfire and unintentional good comes out of his troublemaking.

Trickster tales are frequently funny, but on a deeper level they point up human failings, such as greed and foolishness. They teach moral lessons, showing what happens when envy, lust, or other desires or cravings get out of control. Some trickster tales hold out hope of redemption as well. And sometimes, tricksters, like their foolish, greedy human counterparts, learn from their behavior and become heroes.

Raven of the Northwest Coast

Raven of the Northwest Coast peoples is culture hero and trickster rolled into one. Raven is a huge black bird who can push up his beak and shrug off his wings to take on human form at will. He is revered for his creative powers, and for his basic kindness to humans, whom he watches over and helps.

Some tales credit Raven with creating the earth by dropping pebbles into the sea. In any case, he was the first being on it, responsible for the coming of human life. The Haida, a people of the Northwest Coast, tell how Raven was walking alone on the shore when he found a clam shell. Inside were tiny people. Raven coaxed them out, and they became the ancestors of the Haida tribe. Other peoples came to be in different ways. According to an Inuit tale, the first man emerged from a pea pod

This mural depicts the Haida First People emerging from the clam shell with the help of Raven.

on a vine that Raven had planted after he made the earth. Surveying his world, Raven saw the man and swooped down. The man pushed back Raven's beak, and beneath it, he saw Raven's human face.

Raven could see that man was lonely. So he made another figure from the clay of the stream and breathed life into it. It was the first woman. Together the man and the woman had many children, who lived and grew and peopled the earth.

When Raven plays tricks, he may do it on behalf of humans for whom he feels special affection. It was Raven who brought light to the world when the sun was locked away from people by a powerful chief. By employing his magic, Raven turned himself into a tiny particle in the drinking water of the chief's daughter and was later born to her as a human baby. When he cried for the box that held the sun, the chief gave it to him to hold. Instantly, he turned back into Raven and flew off, carrying the sun back to light the world.

Raven's trickery often led to the creation of some geographical or natural feature. Thus almost everything people see in nature serves as a reminder of Raven and the creation of the world. As with other tricksters, the mistakes Raven made as he went about trying to satisfy his desires often became object lessons in what to avoid.

Probably the best known trickster is Coyote, a half-animal, half-human being who appears in the tales of many cultures. In the Plateau region of the Northwest, he is both trickster and creator. According to the tales of the people there, it is through Coyote's trickery that the salmon, on which they depend for food, travel upstream each year. The Shoshone and Paiute of the Great Basin tell tales in which Coyote is the father of the first people. The Navajo say that Coyote caused the flood that covered the earth before the people emerged from the underworld.

Coyote's tricks sometimes brought him grief. California Indians tell that when Coyote felt there were too many people, he decided that there should be death, only to have his own son be one of the first to die. Coyote tried to take back his decree, but it was too late. To console himself, Coyote established rites for people to use when their loved ones die.

How Things Came to Be

Native American tales often explained the formation of geographical features as supernatural events, frequently as a divine response to the actions of people. In whatever direction Native Americans gazed, whether on the earth or in the sky, what they saw there was related to their sacred history. The world around them was thus a continual reminder of the sacredness beside and within which they lived.

The Nisqually of the Pacific Northwest tell how, when the world was young, the Creator gave the people everything they might need. Even so, two brothers quarreled over land. The Creator took them aside and gave them each a bow and a single arrow. Each shot his arrow, and where it landed, that land became his. The brothers went their separate ways, creating two tribes, the Multnomahs and the Klickitats.

For a long time, the tribes lived apart in peace, their lands joined by a stone bridge over the Columbia River, which they crossed freely. But after a while, each began to covet the other's land. The Creator, unhappy at this turn of events, punished the people by taking away fire and bringing autumn rains. Soon the people were cold and damp. They begged the Creator to return fire to them, promising to give up their quarrelsome ways.

The only fire left was at the lodge of Loo-Wit, an old woman who was always good and not quarrelsome or envious. The Creator offered to grant Loo-Wit any wish she might have if she would agree to share her fire with the people. Loo-Wit agreed to share her fire with the people in return for becoming young and beautiful again.

Soon the people saw a beautiful maiden tending fire at the stone bridge. The two tribes abandoned their silly quarrels and received fire from her, and for a time they lived comfortably and peacefully again. But the chief of each tribe saw the beautiful maiden that Loo-Wit had become. Each wanted her for his wife. Fighting broke out again.

This time, the Creator snatched the two chiefs away and turned them into mountains. The chief of the Klickitats, to the north, became Mount Adams; the Chief of the Multnomahs, to the south, became Mount Hood. Even then they did not stop their rumbling and quarreling, tossing rocks back and forth, almost blocking the river between them. Loo-Wit was unhappy to have caused such suffering. The Creator took pity on her and turned her into a mountain as well.

Most of the time, Loo-Wit sleeps peacefully. But she is a reminder to people to live in peace with their neighbors and keep their hearts free of envy and greed. If they do not, she might awaken and demonstrate her unhappiness. You see, Loo-Wit did not become an ordinary mountain. Because she had always been good, the Creator let her keep her fire. Loo-Wit is the volcano whose other name is Mount Saint Helens.

Like many Native American tales, the story of Loo-Wit not only explains the existence of the volcano, a mountain of fire, but shows the consequences of quarreling and fighting. Native Americans' sacred tales reflect the high standards of behavior they set for all individuals. People, although they often fall short of the ideal, are expected to live in peace with their neighbors and not to be greedy and quarrelsome, to steal, to break taboos, or to fail to listen to the will of the spirits. Bad actions could bring trouble, even disaster, not only to the individual, but to the tribe as a whole. Goodness, charity, and kindness are necessary to maintain balance and harmony in the world, and the oral tradition made people continually aware of that necessity.

The Sacred Pipe of the Lakota

The relationship of people in the here and now to the natural universe is more important in Native American religions than is any sort of historical record. Although tales tell of tribal heroes, the hero was only rarely a historical figure, and usually the focus was not on the hero, but on what the hero did for the tribe—for example, establishing a sacred place or custom, or bringing a sacred object to the tribe.

One of the most sacred of all tribal objects is the sacred pipe of the Lakota. The Lakota, once known as the Teton, the largest and westernmost of the Sioux peoples of the western Plains, depended heavily on the buffalo for food, clothing, and shelter,

---

■ *Seven Sacred Rites of the Lakota*

According to Lakota tradition Buffalo Calf Woman, a spirit messenger from Wakan Tanka, taught the Lakota seven sacred rites of Canku Luta, the Pipe Religion:

Sweat Lodge Ceremony *(Inikagapi). This ceremony prepares the participants for entering and leaving the presence of sacredness.*

Vision Quest *(Hanbleceya). An individual visits an isolated natural place, fasts, and prays for a vision that will provide spiritual guidance.*

Ghost Keeping Ceremony *(Wanagi Yuhapi). A ceremony that holds the soul of someone who has died and purifies it so that it may return pure to Wakan Tanka.*

Hunka Ceremony *(The Making of Relatives). This ceremony establishes a binding relationship among members of the tribe.*

Girl's Puberty Rite *(Isnati Awicalowan). The girl learns her sacred duities and responsibilities as a woman.*

Throwing the Ball Ceremony *(Tapa Wankayeyapi). People try to catch a ball that symbolizes the universe. Their attempts represent the struggle of humans to give up ignorance.*

■ *Black Elk, a nine-teenth-century Lakota religious leader, recorded his religious experiences in the autobiographical* Black Elk Speaks. *His memoirs helped to preserve many Lakota traditions and beliefs that might otherwise have been lost.*

and the animal was sacred to them. They hunted it with respect, trying to take only what was necessary for their lives so there would always be enough. According to legend, the sacred pipe was the gift of the Buffalo People, messengers of the Great Spirit, to the humans who depended on them.

One day, a beautiful woman dressed in white buckskin appeared to two Sioux hunters. Although they recognized her as coming from the spirit world, one of the hunters desired her. When he approached her, a cloud of mist covered them both. When the mist cleared, the woman was as before, but the man whose thoughts about her were impure had been reduced to a skeleton. The woman told the other hunter to go home and tell their chief to prepare for her coming by putting up a special ceremonial lodge. He raced home with the tale, and the people built the lodge as the woman had commanded.

The next morning, the woman appeared. She carried with her a pipe, with the stem in her right hand and the bowl in her left hand. She went into the lodge and took the place of honor. After the chief had welcomed her, she began to speak. She told the people that under Wakan Tanka, all beings were as one family. The Sioux were known to be honorable and respectful of the sacred. She came as a representative of the Buffalo People, who sent the pipe. It was to be used as she directed, to make peace between warring nations and to heal the sick.

Buffalo Calf Woman, as she came to be known, spoke to the women of the Sioux, telling them of the special feeling that Wakan Tanka had for them, and to the children, whom she told to lead pure lives and respect the pipe. Finally she told the men that the pipe was to be used only for good. They must always respect the fruits of the earth. They should help the women in the raising of children and share their sorrows, and be kind to the children. When they needed buffalo meat, they should smoke the pipe, and their hunting would be successful. Finally, she lighted the pipe and offered it to the sky, to the earth, and to the four winds, from which all good things come.

Her message delivered, the woman asked that the way be cleared for her to leave. As she stepped out of the lodge, she turned into a buffalo calf.

To the people of the Plains, the sacred pipe symbolizes the earth and all plant and animal life on it. The bowl represents the earth with all its life-giving properties. The stem is the life on earth, with its energy and strength. When the two parts of the pipe are joined, all of the powers of the earth come together in it.

In smoking the pipe, people are connected to the powers of the universe. Pipe ceremonies were among the most sacred of all rituals, and agreements and pacts made at those times were sacred trusts, considered by all parties to be unbreakable and holy. The custom of the pipe is widespread across North America and continues to this day.

The Variety of the Oral Tradition

Every Native American tribe, large or small, has its own separate, fully developed oral tradition containing dozens, even hundreds of tales. No one knows them all, or even how many there are. Some tales have never been written down or told outside the tribe, because they are considered too sacred for any but tribal ears.

Sacred stories tie all of the things in the natural and spirit world to the life of the tribe. Everything has a story—mountains and rivers, trees and grass, sky and earth, sun, moon, and stars, rainbows and whirlwinds, the foods people eat, the clothes they wear, the deer and the eagle, the rat's tail and the hawk's beak, the infant's cradle board, baskets and blankets, the way homes are built. All of these things are not in themselves sacred, but each has a sacred dimension and all are reminders of the sacredness in life. The oral tradition reinforces this sacredness with each telling and retelling of the tales during a person's lifetime.

CHAPTER 4

Native American Ceremonies and Rituals

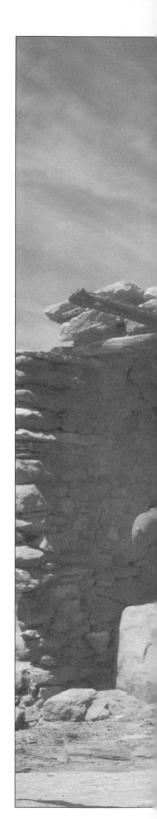

*A*ll Native American religions use dance and drama as a way of communicating with the higher powers of the universe. For Native Americans, dance is a kind of prayer in motion, one that involves the entire body.

When speaking of a dance, Native Americans are referring to more than just patterns of footsteps and body motions, more than events in which a series of dances is performed. A dance is a religious rite. Sacred dance-dramas reenact the tribe's creation beliefs or represent the actions of powerful spirits. They dramatize the relationship between people, the natural world, and the spirit world. Thus there are dances to bring rain, to make corn grow, for good hunting and well-being, and to renew the earth.

Each tribe has its own characteristic form of dance. In the eastern woodlands, people dance as a group, usually in a circle that moves counterclockwise. On the Plains, the tribes developed many styles—circle dances, line dances, solo dances. Tribes of the Southwest use both circle dances and line dances. In the Northwest and among the Inuit, solo dances are more common than group dances. Both men and women dance, although usually separately and at different times. Dancers perform not for themselves alone but for the whole tribe. In this way they bring the power of the spirit world to all.

The kind of dance a tribe developed reflected its character and view of the world. Tribes that depended mainly on hunting, for example, had dances that called on the spirits of their game, such as buffalo or deer. Tribes whose livelihood came principally from farming performed rites celebrating the agricultural cycle of growth and harvest. A dance takes place in a special performance area, often one that is selected by ritual means and sanctified for the purpose of the dance. Where weather is reliable, the site is usually outdoors, in a field or meadow. On the rainy Northwest Coast, the Kwakiutl build special dance houses in which to hold their ceremonies.

The spiritual power of the dance is so strong that according to Native American belief the dancer does not simply perform the role of a spirit but is said to *personate* the spirit, or become a living embodiment of the spirit depicted by a mask or costume. Through that mask or costume, the spirit the dancer represents is believed to enter into the body of the dancer, thus linking the human and the supernatural worlds.

Masks and Costumes

In Native American dance, the dancers wear elaborate masks and costumes representing the spirit world and charged with sacred significance. Each part of a costume has symbolic meaning. For the Pueblo corn dance, for example, a ceremony for rain and the health and well-being of the community, a male Pueblo dancer wears a white cotton kilt embroidered with symbols of the clouds and rain and tied with a white, tasseled rain sash. A fox skin, a reminder of the common ancestry of humans and animals, hangs from the belt. Behind the dancer's right knee is tied a turtle-shell rattle, and he carries a gourd rattle in his right hand to make the sound of falling rain. On his moccasins is skunk fur to protect him from evil. A sash worn diagonally across his left shoulder is decorated with shells from the Pacific Ocean, the great water. On his head, he wears a cluster of parrot feathers to bring rain from the south, and he carries sprigs of evergreen, a symbol of greenery and life.

On the Northwest Coast, dancers wear large, stylized wooden masks that depict the raven and other creatures of the area—whales, seals, bears—as well as monsters and other kinds of spirits as they dance out the themes of creation and the opposition of natural forces.

Animal Dances

Nearly all tribes pay homage to animal spirits with dances that imitate an animal's traits or movements. Hunting dances, which recognized the animals people hunted to survive, were once widely held to honor the animals and to call on the spirits to increase their numbers, as well as to gain the cooperation of the animal spirits so that hunters would be able to take the game they needed.

■ *This mask and robe, worn in ceremonies, represent the spirit of the halibut, an important food fish for the Northwest Coast tribes.*

Many costumes depicted animals, such as antelope and deer, and even fish. On the Plains, buffalo dancers honored the animal whose body gave them food, fuel, clothing, and shelter. These dancers wore elaborate costumes that included a buffalo mask and horns, a buffalo (skin) robe, and a tail. Buffalo dances were not limited to the Plains, however. Among Pueblo peoples, the buffalo was believed to have the power to cure illness. After a dance, a dancer would touch the sick with the buffalo head-dress to effect a cure.

The eagle was sacred to many native peoples because of its strength, its fierceness, and its ability to soar higher than any other bird. In the Southwest, the eagle brought rain. Eagle dances, which incorporate soaring and swooping motions, called on the eagle in its role as messenger to the Great Spirit to carry the prayers of the people aloft.

In modern times, with fewer people depending on hunting and game for their livelihood, fewer animal ceremonies occur. In the Northwest, however, people still observe the running of the salmon with traditional rites, and the Inuit still honor the seal, whales, and other animals of the far North with traditional rites. Individual Native American hunters of all areas often observe rites before, during, and after the hunt to ensure successful hunting and win the cooperation of the game. A hunter may offer tobacco, corn meal, and a prayer feather to newly killed game. The dead game is treated with respect, and its bones are disposed of ceremonially.

Kachinas

Among the most intricate and sacred costumes are the kachina costumes of the Hopi and other tribes of the Southwest. *Kachinas* are the deified ancestral spirits from whom the Hopi learned their rituals and customs when they first emerged from the underworld. Each kachina—and there are hundreds of them—has a specific set of stylized characteristics that readily identify it to watchers. Kachinas contain many symbols of the natural world. They represent both animal and plant spirits, as well as the spirit beings of the sky and the sun, the weather, war, monsters, sacred clowns, and many others. Because they

Kachinas, the spirits that watch over the Hopi and communicate with the higher powers, are represented by carved figures as well as by the masks and costumes of kachina dancers.

represent the spirit world, they are not meant to be realistic. A kachina's hair, for example, may be represented by wheat, feathers, or flowers, or it may be cut to indicate falling rain; the face may be a rainbow, an animal's snout, or a pattern of lines and symbols. The kachina also carries or wears special identifying objects, such as the skin of a particular animal, a blanket of a distinctive design, weapons, musical instruments, or plants.

The Hopi believe that a dancer who wears a kachina costume and mask receives the spirit of that kachina. Through the kachina dancer, the prayers of the people are carried more quickly to the higher powers of the universe.

Sacred Music

For Native Americans, music has supernatural power. A sacred song can carry prayers to the spirit world, cure illness, and influence weather and events. In the words of the Lakota holy man Red Weasel, "I may pray with my mouth and the prayer will be heard, but if I sing it will be heard sooner by

Wakan Tanka." Almost all Native American ceremonies are accompanied by music, especially drumming, "the heartbeat of mother earth." Other instruments commonly used in ceremonies are flutes, pipes, and rattles.

Although Native American music is rhythmic, the rhythm is often irregular, more like a speech rhythm or the rhythm of bird song than the regular beat of European or Western music. And while some cultures use a musical scale that is similar to that of Western music, other traditions make use of speech tones, with intervals too small to be played on a standard keyboard. These qualities help to give Native American music its unusual and distinctive sound.

Musical instruments used in ceremonies are often considered sacred objects because they are used to call on the higher powers of the universe. They are made ritually and cared for with respect. Drums are made by stretching an animal skin over a frame or by hollowing out a section of log. Water drums, which have a distinctive tone, are clay or metal containers partly filled with water and covered with an animal skin. Drums are ordinarily played with a stick or sticks, rather than with bare hands. Rattles may be made with hollow objects, such as gourds, hollow sticks, or turtle shells, filled with pebbles, or of objects such as deer hooves or shells strung together. The human voice is also used to accompany rituals, in sacred chants and songs or as a kind of background.

Most traditional songs of Native Americans had a definite purpose, and often the purpose was prayer. If a woman sang as she was grinding corn, the song was probably a prayer for rain or good harvest. A lullaby is not just a soothing tune but words with the power to bring sleep. Other groups have specific songs for hunting or for healing. Many tribes have songs to influence the weather. Most Pueblo songs, for example, are prayers for rain. Along the Northwest Coast, there are songs to quiet storms and rough waters.

Each tribe has its own musical tradition. To the Navajo, songs and music are so sacred that they are reserved for ritual use—particularly in healing ceremonies, which are called "sings." Music is considered too spiritually powerful to be used casually. The Navajo also use song for protection, or "cover," from harmful spirits. When someone is singing, no evil can come within hearing range of the song. The Navajo are only one of many groups who refer to their holy people, or shamans, as "singers."

Shamans and holy people of all tribes learn songs and chants that enable them to contact the spirit world. Some shamans use the rhythmic sounds of the drum to aid them in falling into a trance. The most sacred songs are never sung except during religious rituals and are heard only by the initiated or by those for whom the ritual is being conducted.

In tribes with a tradition of vision quests for guardian spirits, one outcome of the quest is often a personal song. Individual dreamers receive songs in their visions and sing them throughout their lives to call on spirit power for personal success. A song that comes through a vision is considered the singer's personal property and is not sung by others.

■ The drum, "the heartbeat of Mother Earth," is an important ceremonial instrument in many of the Native American traditions. Here, drummers from Santa Clara Pueblo in New Mexico join together during a feast day.

The Sweat Lodge Ceremony

The Sweat Lodge Ceremony, called by the Lakota the *Inikagapi,* is almost universal among North American Indian tribes. It is a form of ritual purification that precedes important ceremonies and dances. It may be part of a ceremony for health and healing. It is both a religious rite and an essential part of the Native American tradition, during which cultural beliefs and practices are handed down to the next generation.

A sweat lodge is usually a small structure made of young trees that can be easily bent into a dome shape. The framework is covered with blankets or animal hides. It sits directly on the ground, over a hole dug in the center. It is usually big enough to hold six or seven people. Generally, there are separate sweat ceremonies for men and women.

■ *A Lakota medicine man adds hot coals to a sweat lodge.*

During a sweat, a spiritual leader heats rocks in a fire built outside the lodge and then places them in the hole inside. The rocks themselves are sacred, chosen for their ability to tolerate and hold heat. The leader pours water over the rocks to make steam, a symbol of the breath of life. He or she may also add sacred herbs. To regulate the heat, he or she can let in fresh air by lifting the coverings on the lodge. During the ceremony, he or she offers songs and prayers for healing the participants or for the health and well-being of the tribe or the world. Animal spirits are believed to come to the sweat, and spirit power is present throughout the ceremony.

World Renewal

Most Native American groups celebrate world renewal ceremonies, annual rituals for maintaining order and harmony in the world. World renewal celebrates the creation of the cosmos and the beginning of time. Through ritual and ceremony, people return to their origins, seeking to recapture the purity and power of the newly created world.

World renewal ceremonies differ from tribe to tribe. Tribal groups with hunting and military cultures, such as the Lakota and the Shoshone of the western Plains, had world renewal practices that emphasized courage and endurance. People who relied more on farming, such as the Pueblo and the Seminole, centered their rites on fertility and growth. Tribes in California, where earthquakes are common, performed a yearly rite to stabilize the universe.

The Sun Dance

As many as thirty different Native American groups of the Plains and the prairie celebrate a festival during which they pray and perform sacrifices for the renewal of the world and the people, give thanks for the blessings of the past year, and attempt through prayer and devotion to bring all things into balance and harmony for the year to come. The Shoshone and the Crow call their ceremony the Thirst Lodge; the Arapaho, the Offerings Lodge; and the Cheyenne, the New Life Lodge; but it is best known by its Lakota name, the Dance Gazing at the Sun, or the

Sun Dance. The Sun Dance is the most important religious festival celebrated by the native people of the Plains today. It usually takes place in the spring or around the summer solstice, the time when the sun is highest in the sky, or in midsummer.

The dance takes place in the center of the encampment, which represents the center of the earth. A tall pole in the center of the encampment represents the world tree that connects all the powers of heaven, earth, and the underworld. The pole, from a freshly cut tree, is prepared and decorated ritually.

A lodge is constructed, with the tree as its center. The building of the lodge is a ritual that represents the creation of the world, and while the lodge stands, it is believed to hold within it the power of the newly created universe. The entry faces east, the direction of the rising sun. The lodge is open to the sky; piles of brush around the outside lend privacy to the dancers.

The Sun Dance begins with acts of purification and sacrifice. Young men who are going to take part in the dance are ritually purified in a Sweat Lodge Ceremony and observe a total fast, going without food and water for three or four days. Dancers move for one complete day along the inside edge of the lodge from east to west, turning around the pole so they are always facing the sun. They remain within the lodge for the duration of the ceremony, fasting, praying, and dancing. Often they receive a sacred vision in the course of the dance.

In the Lakota tradition, participants in the Sun Dance demonstrated their self-sacrifice with flesh piercing, an ordeal they believed would bring them closer to spiritual revelation. A spiritual leader inserted skewers, or sharpened sticks, under the skin and muscle of the dancer's chest. Long strips of rawhide leather were tied to the skewers and to the central pole, and thus attached, the dancer performed to the point of exhaustion. A similar practice pierced the dancer's back and shoulders. Only a few tribes employed piercing; others deliberately rejected it. Kiowa belief, for example, forbade shedding blood during their Sun Dance ceremony. Piercing is rare today, although some Lakota still do it.

The Shoshone Sun Dance ceremony includes rituals conducted at sunup by a spiritual leader. The men and women dancers move together to a drumbeat, singing a greeting to the rising sun. They catch the sun's first rays on eagle feathers that are tied to their wrists, and they touch the feathers to their bodies as a sign of purity and power. Sacred songs and prayers complete the rite. On the third day, people who are ill come to the lodge to be healed by the spiritual leader. The ceremony concludes at the end of the fourth day, when the leaders bring the dancers water that has been ritually blessed. Gifts and feasting follow.

Corn Dances

In agricultural areas, people developed rituals and ceremonies to deal with crops and the weather. Native Americans believe that prayer and attention to the spirits can influence the spirit world and therefore nature. Most agricultural tribes performed a ritualistc dance to bring life-giving rain. Other tribes had corn ceremonies and planting rituals.

A ceremony shared by many agricultural peoples is the Green Corn Dance, a major ceremony in which the people give thanks to the creator and all spirits for the year's bounty. It is usually held when the first corn is ripe. Among the Iroquois of the Northeast, the ceremony is held in late August. Among the Oklahoma Seminole and Creek, it is held in late June or early July, and among the Shawnee, in July or August.

The Green Corn Dance: Seminole

For the Seminole of Oklahoma, the Green Corn Dance, or Stomp Dance, is the most important event of their ritual year. In keeping with the theme of world renewal, it is a time when medicine bundles are refurbished and a new year begins.

In traditional practice, all corn from the previous harvest is used up, and a time of renewal and purification is begun. Homes are cleaned and old utensils replaced. The men of the tribe gather to discuss and resolve any disputes of the past year. All crimes except the most serious may be forgiven at this time, and anyone who has been sent away from the tribe as a punishment can return home. During this period, the men participate in Sweat Lodge Ceremonies, fast, and drink an herbal drink that causes them to vomit, symbolically ridding them of the old year and purifying their bodies for the beginning of the new one. There is

Corn dancers from Santa Clara Pueblo, New Mexico, participate in an annual festival to bring rain and good fortune in the coming year.

also a Seminole tradition of "scratching," in which boys and men, and sometimes girls as well, are scratched on the chest, arms, and legs, formerly with owl claws, and now with needles. This, too, is a form of purification. According to Seminole belief, badness flows out in the blood from the scratches, and goodness remains within.

The ceremony includes several traditional dances—Stomp, Long, Ribbon, Feather, and Buffalo. The Stomp Dance itself is a sacred ceremony, considered to be health-giving and renewing. Dancers who are in good physical condition may dance continuously for two or three hours.

The Green Corn Dance is a time for ball games, and competition may be fierce. The special roles of males and females in the society are recognized, and there are coming-of-age and naming ceremonies for children. Other features of the dance are "going to water," or ritual bathing, and prayer. The ceremony ends with a final ball game and breakfast.

The Corn Dance: Pueblo

Among the Pueblo people, who celebrate it in late spring or early summer, the ritual Corn Dance is held to bring life-giving rain. The ceremony combines song, drama, dance, and poetry to pray for rain, harvest, the health and growth of all plant and animal life, and the well-being of the people.

For the Corn Dance, the people of a pueblo are divided into two groups: the Squash, or "winter" people, and the Turquoise, or "summer" people. Dancers wear blue or yellow body paint to indicate their group.

First in the procession come dancers representing the *Koshare* and the *Kurena,* the spirit beings who taught the people how to make crops grow. They lead a procession of the chorus, which may number fifty or more. Throughout the ceremony, the people of the chorus serve as sacred clowns, mocking the actions of the other dancers and bringing laughter. After the chorus come the corn dancers, led by a man carrying a long pole that symbolizes the world tree the people climbed to emerge from the underworld. The pole is decorated with a sun symbol and a banner, which he waves over them to symbolize rain clouds.

The Squash dancers and the Turquoise dancers alternate throughout the day, performing complicated dances that are the centerpiece of the ceremony. At the end of the day, all groups join the chorus for a final display.

Sacred Clowns

People are foolish. They behave in inappropriate and thoughtless ways, out of step, out of place, out of proportion. This aspect of being human is represented in Native American religions by a figure called a sacred clown.

Sacred clowns appear in many Native American ceremonies, particularly in the Southwest. They can be seen alongside processions, two beats behind everyone else, tripping, poking the dancers, making improper gestures at the observers, and generally provoking amusement and outright laughter. They may be men dressed as women or in costumes with grossly exaggerated body parts. They mimic sacred rituals, only to get them wrong. The Lakota *heyoka,* or clown, rides horseback, but when he jumps on the horse, he is facing backwards. Sacred clowns are wise as well as foolish, however. Like other supernatural beings, they have sacred powers. In some traditions, for example, it is the clowns who intercede with the higher spirits to bring rain.

In Native American regions, clowns do things that people are afraid to do. They thumb their noses at propriety to keep people from becoming rigid and self-righteous. They hold up a mirror to human foolishness. People laugh, but they also learn. The clowns dramatize the pitfalls of life's path and remind people that laughter is indeed a sacred and spiritual gift.

The Ritual Year

Many tribes followed a calendar of ceremonies that celebrated the renewal of the Earth. The Shoshone held four festivals, the first in late winter, anticipating the disappearance of snow and the return of life. A second festival came at planting, which also followed ritual. A Sun Dance was performed in summer, and a harvest festival was held in the autumn.

The Hopi ritual year begins in November with *Wuwuchim*, a sacred ceremony that reenacts the people's emergence from the underworld. Leaders ritually close all roads to the village with sacred corn meal, except the road to the burial ground. All lights and fires are extinguished, and the dead are invited to return. Then a new fire is kindled and distributed to each house.

In December, the Hopi celebrate the winter solstice, the time when the days begin to lengthen again. *Kivas*, the sacred ceremonial chambers of the Hopi, are ritually opened so that the kachinas, or spirits, can enter. Men who belong to kachina societies dress in kachina costumes to perform sacred dances. During January, there is much traditional dancing. The kachinas visit children and give them presents or, if they have misbehaved, warn them to mend their ways. Older children are initiated into kachina societies and learn the secrets of the kachinas during this time.

Beginning in April, more kachina dances are held. Their purpose is to bring rain; to promote harmony in the universe; and to ensure health, long life, and happiness. Then, just before the summer solstice in June, a sixteen-day ceremonial series called *Niman* completes the kachina season. Different ceremonies alternate during Niman. Some years it is the flute ceremony, a reenactment of the emergence story, which also brings rain and good harvest. On alternate years, dancers perform the Snake Dance, which reenacts the legend of a young Hopi who married a woman of the Snake People, and who was able to bring rain to his people during a drought. At the end of the Niman festival, the kachinas return to their homes in the sky to await the coming of the next kachina season.

Ritual and Prayer in Native American Life

Native American ritual and prayer are as richly varied and diverse as the many Native American cultures from which they come. In some cultures, prayer is spontaneous, simply "speaking" to a particular spirit or to the Great Spirit. Other cultures, especially in the Southwest, memorize prayers that must be recited exactly in order to reach the spirit world effectively. As with everything else in Native American religion, there is no single way of praying. But for native peoples, prayer is much more than the spoken word. All life is prayer.

Ritual cycles carry Native Americans though the calendar year with celebrations that link them to the natural world: the unresting path of the sun, stars, and moon, the creatures that walk and fly and crawl on the earth and swim in the sea, the plant life from which come food and healing herbs and shade and materials for building and creating the objects of daily life. Their colorful and stylized rituals, made up of dance, song, prayer, music, sacrifice, and offering, are a recurring reminder of their indebtedness to mother earth, the spirit world, and the Great Spirit itself.

CHAPTER 5

Wholeness and Healing

Native American thought places great emphasis on wholeness and wellness. Human health, for both the individual and the group, depends on proper actions and interactions with the spirit world. Well-being comes about through walking in harmony with the forces of nature and the universe. By contrast, illness is a sign of having fallen out of step with those forces. Curing takes place through rituals that restore the sick person to balance and harmony.

Many Native American celebrations have a curing or healing component. World renewal ceremonies, which call on the higher powers to restore the earth and to bring health and well-being to the tribe as a whole, may also be times of individual healing. The Lakota Sun Dance, for example, includes a time when people who are sick can enter the sacred circle and receive its power for healing. Dancers often dedicate their participation to physical or emotional healing for themselves or someone close to them.

Causes of Illness

According to traditional beliefs, illness comes from supernatural forces. The Cherokee, for example, believe that animal spirits bring illness to hunters who do not pay the proper respect to game they kill. Careless hunting by one person can bring disease to the hunter or to the entire tribe. Other groups believe that bad actions, such as ignoring taboos, cause internal problems. The Iroquois attribute illnesses to unfulfilled desires and dreams. Among some Inuit tribes, illness can be the result of sins committed by ancestors.

People may also become ill because of contact with evil spirits. An evil spirit may come from a spell cast by a witch or a sorcerer—sometimes an evil shaman—or from someone who wishes the sufferer ill. One cause of illness is called object intrusion. An evil spirit sends illness in the form of a foreign object, such as a stone or a bone, that enters a person's body. Symptoms of object intrusion include internal pain or injury.

In addition, serious illness may be the result of "soul loss," in which evil spirits, especially those of the dead, capture the sick person's soul when it is out of his or her body during sleep. A diagnosis of soul loss denotes critical illness. The patient may have a wasting disease, be delirious, unconscious, or in a coma.

The Role of the Shaman

Native Americans consider healing a sacred calling. Not all people have the gift to become healers, but those who do must use it, or they may themselves become sick by failing to do what the spirits call them to do. Native healers have used healing places and natural means to cure their people for thousands of years. Healing power comes from the natural forces of the earth, which can be reached through prayer.

Today, with the wide availability of modern medicine, most Native Americans go to doctors when they are sick. They may also consult a shaman, a holy person honored as a medicine man or woman, for a healing ceremony. Native American healing rituals are a form of alternative medicine that many Native Americans—and some nonnative people as well—use in combination with Western medicine. In remote areas, such as the

■ *An Alaskan shaman, photographed in Alaska in 1904, displays his mask, wand, and rattle, all part of the healing ceremony.*

arctic and subarctic regions, where access to modern medicine may be limited, people still consult shamans and medicine people for many of their medical needs. Although in general people no longer rely entirely on shamans and medicine people for healing, individuals are still called by the spirits to become healers. Most tribes have members who have studied traditional Native American healing practices and conduct healing ceremonies.

Shamans receive their powers from their ties to the world of the spirits—some through dreams and visions or in a vision quest, others through study. All, however, share the ability to see visions or to enter into a trance to receive instructions from the spirits. In tribes of the North and Northwest, the shaman prepares himself by fasting and praying, singing, and drumming until he falls into a trance, a sign of his soul having left his body. The shaman's guardian spirits then speak, telling him what the cause of disease is and if and how it can be cured. Not all illnesses are curable. After diagnosing the cause of the illness, the shaman performs the proper ritual for curing it, usually with the help of a spirit. The ritual involves combinations of charms, songs, and healing herbs.

Even before the coming of modern medicine, the shaman's ceremonies were usually reserved for serious medical problems with spiritual or supernatural causes. Shamans specialized in curing particular illnesses. Someone with an internal ailment would go to a shaman known for curing that kind of problem and consult a different shaman for a sore that would not heal. In addition to serious illness, shamans dealt with such injuries as broken bones and snakebite. Many had a broad knowledge of healing herbs as well.

Traditionally, not all native healers were shamans, a role that required not only special spiritual gifts but also many years of study. Someone with a simple ailment, such as an upset stomach or a headache, might consult a herbalist, a specialist in the use of plants as medicine, just as he or she would probably see a family doctor or pick up something at the drugstore today.

Herbalists were also considered to have received their gifts from the spirit world, and they often consulted those spirits to decide which herb to prescribe.

Although healers are often called medicine men, many tribes have medicine women as well. In some tribes, the shaman is usually a woman. The Lakota have had many medicine women who showed their calling from an early age. In general, though, women do not become medicine people until the end of their childbearing years because menstrual blood is deemed to have special powers of its own.

 A Lakota medicine man conducts a Pipe Ceremony after a sacred walk.

Healing Rituals

Different tribes have developed different healing rituals, many of which are so sacred that they are never photographed or recorded. Plains tribes have special sacred objects and talismans that they might use along with incantations to cure illness. Among the Tohono O'odham of Arizona, those who believe that illnesses are caused by improper behavior toward animal spirits, treat patients with fetishes—small, carved animal forms. The healer chooses a fetish of the animal that is believed to have healing properties for a particular illness, and presses it to the part of the body that is afflicted to draw off harmful influences. The fetish for kidney and stomach problems, for example, is a snake; for rheumatism and foot sores, a horned toad; for children's fevers, a Gila monster (poisonous lizard).

■ On the Pine Ridge Indian Reservation in South Dakota, a medicine man spreads sage on what will be the floor of a sweat lodge for ritual purification.

Other native groups rely on the power of animal spirits in other ways. Bear power is considered a powerful healing force by Lakota, Anishinabe (Chippewa), and Pueblo peoples, and their shamans frequently wore bearskins or masks.

If a disease is caused by object intrusion, the object must be located and removed. The healer seeks a vision that shows where the object is, and then removes it by sucking, blowing, or rubbing the patient's skin. Sometimes the shaman produces the object that caused the problem—usually a bone, stone, feather, or other small item—for the patient and any observers to see.

A Lakota Healing Ceremony

Among the Lakota, the power to cure illness is a gift that comes in a personal vision from the Great Spirit. Thus healing ceremonies are highly individual. The ceremony requires objects with spirit power: a sacred pipe; a drum, a rattle, and a whistle for summoning spirits; water that has been blessed; and herbs. The healer sings songs received in a vision, often while touching the afflicted part of the patient's body. Throughout the ceremony, the healer calls on the spirits to cure the patient and reinforces the belief that the patient will be cured.

A typical healing ritual begins with a Sweat Lodge Ceremony and the cooking of foods for a ritual feast. After the sweat, everyone moves indoors, where the room has been emptied of furniture. Typically, friends and relatives of the sick person come to participate in the ceremony, because the health of each member of the tribe is important to the whole community.

Assistants hang draperies over the windows and doors to make the room dark. Objects of steel and glass and such things as mirrors and pictures are removed or covered. Spirits may appear as light, and reflective surfaces are hostile to them. People also remove their glasses and jewelry.

The healer constructs an altar on a bed of sand that has been laid down for the purpose. The objects on the altar and the sacred fence that surrounds it are assembled according to the instructions of the healer's spirit helpers. Each has its own sacred significance. A sacred fence might be made of as many as five hundred tiny bundles of tobacco in squares of colored cloth representing the directions of the four winds, and Mother Earth and Father Sky.

The holy person purifies the room with smoke from coals from the sacred fire in the sweat lodge, to which herbs have been added. Then the pipe stem and bowl are joined, bringing spirit power to the altar. The healer fills the pipe and makes offerings to the directions of the four winds. In one variation of the ceremony, the healer is bound hand and foot, wrapped in blankets, and laid on the alter. Assistants sing to call the spirits, which observers see as tiny sparks of light and hear as animal or other noises. The patient prays for a cure, and all those assembled in the room pray aloud as well, for the patient's cure and for the well-being of all. The assistants sing curing songs. During this time, the spirits untie the holy person and reveal their instructions. The healer may instruct the patient in spiritual matters or life changes or prescribe herbal medicines. The spirits are thanked, and they depart.

The assistants light the lights. The pipe is passed from hand to hand, and as it passes, each person repeats the words *Mitakuye' Oyasin*, "All of creation are my relatives." Next, water, the source of all life, is passed around. The ceremony ends when the pipe and water have returned to the healer. The altar is taken

---

■ *Navajo Chant*

Navajo ceremonies end with a passage that describes the state of grace and balance to which the participants have returned as a result of the ceremony.

The world before me is restored in beauty
The world behind me is restored in beauty
The world above me is restored in beauty
The world below me is restored in beauty
all things around me are restored in beauty
It is finished in beauty
It is finished in beauty
It is finished in beauty
It is finished in beauty.

from *Navajo Sandpainting Art*, by Eugene Batsoslanii Joe and Mark Bahti, Treasure Chest Publications, Inc. 1978.

down. Small food offerings are made to the four winds and then to Mother Earth and Wakan Tanka. Finally, the people feast on the foods cooked for the ritual meal.

Navajo Chantways

The Navajo believe that illness and misfortune are caused by loss of balance and harmony, usually as the result of wrong behavior or thought. Health and well-being can be restored by a return to the state of harmony that existed at the beginning of the Navajo world, when holy people walked the earth. Navajo rituals are conducted to maintain or restore *hozho,* or harmony, to individuals who suffer from illness or who have wandered from the path of beauty and balance.

Navajo rituals are called chantways. Conducted by a Navajo spiritual leader called a *ha'athali,* or singer, with as many as twelve assistants, a chantway lasts from one to nine days. Except for the Blessingway, a general ritual for restoring harmony to the earth, all chantways are performed for healing.

Chantways are a combination of prayers, songs, herbal medicines, and offerings. There are over fifty chantway rituals, each so complex that it takes years for a singer to master even one, and few singers ever learn more than two. Specific chantways are used for specific diseases. The Shootingway is sung for lung and gastrointestinal ailments. The Beadway is a cure for skin diseases. The Windway is sung for many ailments, including eye problems, heart trouble, and even alcoholism. The Earthway is for women's reproductive health. The Nightway cures mental problems.

At the center of each chantway is a series of sacred designs, called sand paintings, that the ha'athali creates from memory with finely ground colored sand. Navajo ritual sand paintings are so sacred that they are never photographed, although approximate copies of their designs are sometimes made for study or woven into rugs.

Sand paintings depict Navajo holy people, or *yei,* who represent the higher forces of the universe. The ritual calls on the yei to restore the sick person to balance and health. The forces of creation that produced the Navajo world are present in the ritual, drawn there by the singer's creation of the sand painting. The particular paintings that are used emphasize the particular force responsible for the patient's complaint.

The singer prepares the floor of the patient's *hogan*, the simple Navajo dwelling that is also a sacred structure modeled after the homes built by the First People, with a layer of sand. He then creates the painting by trickling colored sand from his hand to form the images of the yei and sprinkles cornmeal on the painting to summon the spirits. The patient, ritually bathed and dried with cornmeal, a sacred substance, is painted with sacred symbols of the spirits.

The patient walks into the sand painting and sits in its center, facing east, the direction of blessing. Sitting within the sacred universe and surrounded by the spirits, the patient actually becomes a part of the painting. The singer touches parts of the painting and the patient's body, uniting the patient with the painting. In this way, the singer transfers the power of the painting to the sick person and enables the healing power of the yei to enter the person's body.

The ceremony destroys the painting. The bad influences that caused the illness are taken up by the sand. When the sand is ritually removed, evil influences and imbalance go with it, and the awareness of the beauty and harmony of life that the patient receives from the ritual makes healing possible.

In the Navajo tradition, relatives and friends come to the ceremony, not just as observers, but as participants. They chant and pray for the patient's return to health and may also receive medicines along with the patient, symbolically strengthening the power of the experience and sharing in the cure.

Medicine Societies

The Algonquin peoples of the Great Lakes region have what is known as a "Medicine Lodge" tradition. The lodge, a building in which the rituals are conducted, has sacred power itself. It is constructed to represent the universe, facing east and west, with a pole representing the world tree, around which the universe revolves, in its center. As a rule, anyone can join a medicine society to learn its mysteries. Among the Ojibwa, people join the *Midewiwin,* or Grand Medicine Society, to learn to communicate with plant spirits in order to select the proper herbs to cure disease. People who are ill themselves often join in the hopes of finding a cure.

The Medicine Society has four levels. At the first, most basic level, initiates study healing plants, curing rites, sacred history, and healing powers. They learn the medicine dance that puts them in touch with healing forces and strengthens their own life force. To reach the fourth level of the society takes many years of study. Those who master the most difficult healing arts are the full-fledged shamans.

The Gift of Healing Herbs

Not all illnesses that require doctoring, of course, are the result of supernatural intrusion or evil spirits. Common complaints, such as fevers, stomach aches, cuts and bruises, muscle strains, and even broken bones have been treated effectively by native healers for centuries. These healers, too, call on the spirit world for help in curing their patients.

Native peoples consider medicinal plants and herbs to be gifts from the spirit world. According to a Cherokee tale, animals and people once lived together and spoke the same language. Then people multiplied rapidly and began to hunt animals for food. The angry deer spirits got together and decided that they would bring disease to people who did not respect them and honor their deaths. But the plant spirits took pity on the people and offered themselves for healing.

Cherokee healers can call on more than four hundred species of wild plants for medicinal purposes. The black-eyed Susan, for example, has multiple uses: its root can be brewed into a tea or made into a paste to treat earache, sores, and snakebite. The healer accompanies the use of the herb with songs and chants to complete the cure.

Plants used as medicine are gathered and prepared according to ritual. Lenape, or Delaware, medicine men and women are individuals who have seen visions that give them a special relationship to the plant world. After a Lenape healer sees a patient, he or she prays for guidance, offering a pinch of tobacco to each of the four winds, then goes to find the plant. When it is located, the healer makes a new offering of tobacco, this time by placing it on the stalk of the healing plant to increase the plant's power. The healer never gathers the first plant of a species, but leaves it to show respect and chooses another.

The ritual for preparing the plant includes drying it in the sun, because the sun's rays add strength. If water is added to make a tea or drink, the water comes from a stream, because the spirits of running water are stronger than those of a lake or pond. Once the medicine has been prepared, the healer administers it with prayers.

Healing the Earth

Healing rituals may be held not just for the healing of people, but for the healing of the earth. Where people have misused the land or polluted air and water, the spirits that give the earth its life and power die out. Prayers to the earth help to return to its natural spiritual state. A holy person may call on spirits to return balance and harmony to a place, to heal the land, cause the water to cleanse itself, and healthy vegetation to grow.

Native Ritual and Modern Medicine

Today, Native Americans regularly avail themselves of Western medicine, but they often seek the help of shamans, or holy people, as well, to help them heal by spiritual means. In recent years, as more Native American young people go into the medical professions, Native Americans who have both medical degrees and an understanding of native practices work successfully to combine the two methods of healing, each of which complements the other. Other doctors may also work in conjunction with native healers in treating their Native American patients.

Spiritual healing is especially important for peoples who have traditionally attributed sickness to a failure to live in harmony with the spirits or to listen to what the spirits and the creator tell them. Behavior does not have to be bad or sinful to cause illness; sickness can come about simply by ignoring the spirits' will. Returning to a spiritual place and listening to the spirits is therefore an important step in becoming well again.

Present-day Shoshone healers conduct the Sweat Lodge Ceremonies that have been used for centuries to cure illness as well as for ritual purification. They believe that the heat of the sweat lodge, along with the sacred elements of rock, water, herbs, prayer, and song, rid the body of impurities that cause illness. The Sweat Lodge Ceremony is considered to be more effective than herbal medicines alone, because of the presence of spirits, particularly animal spirits such as bear, buffalo, or eagle, at the ceremony.

Where a ceremony is held can strengthen its effectiveness. Certain places within each tribe's ancestral lands often have special spiritual power that can be called on for healing. The Shoshone have returned to Rock Creek Canyon in Nevada for centuries because of the healing properties there. Spirit power resides in the entire canyon. One particularly powerful site is Eagle Rock, an outcropping shaped like an eagle's head. After ritual prayer, patients lie on the rock so that the healing power of the eagle can flow into them. The canyon water, too, has healing powers. Sick people who immerse themselves in the waters are believed to leave their illness behind; the flowing water has the power to cleanse itself and become pure again.

Healing through the Mind

Native healers have assembled a vast knowledge of healing techniques and medicinal plants, but according to traditional belief, medicinal herbs are most effective in combination with prayer and ritual. All native healing rituals rely on the influence of the mind on the body, an area that Western medicine has only recently begun to explore. Ceremony and prayer have been used effectively as the major means of healing in native cultures throughout time. As one native healer explains, "A miracle can happen, but in order for it to happen, you are the one who is going to have to allow it—in your mind."

CHAPTER 6

The Path of Life

*I*n native religions, life is a path that has no beginning and no end, always leading back to the starting point. In old age, people are closer to the Great Spirit than at any time since birth. Each individual may travel the path only once, but for the tribe as a whole, life is a continuous cycle of birth, naming, childhood, adolescence, marriage, child-rearing, old age, and death. It is the same path that the first people on earth traveled, and people have followed it since the beginning of time.

The path of life is a spiritual journey, not just a physical one. The ceremonies marking life's passages vary widely from tribe to tribe, but most groups value each stage of life and mark it with ritual and celebration.

Naming Ceremonies

Children represent the future, and throughout Native American cultures, each new life is greatly prized. Mothers-to-be observe taboos and rituals to guarantee healthy babies. Parents and family members make sure to start newborn children on the sacred path, so that they will have long and successful lives. Naming ceremonies make a baby a full member of the tribe and welcome it into the larger community.

Four days after its birth, a Tewa baby's "cord-cutting moth-er," the woman who assisted at its birth, carries it outside to see the dawn for the first time. She uses a small broom to make sweeping motions around the child, gathering the spirits. Then she holds the child up to each of the six directions—north, south, east, and west, up to the sky and down to the earth—and offers a prayer to the forces of the universe. Then she speaks its name, making it a person of the tribe. This ritual starts the child on the *poeh,* the path of life that the first Tewa ancestors walked when they emerged onto the earth.

The Zuni ritual for a new baby occurs on the eighth day, when women of its father's family wash the baby's head and take it outdoors to see the sun rise in the east. They sprinkle corn meal in the breeze and pray for the baby's long life and well-being. The Hopi have a similar ritual, which occurs on the baby's twentieth day.

In the Northwest, the Haida and the Kwakiutl, among oth-ers, bestow names at a "potlatch," or ceremonial feast. A potlatch is held by a family to celebrate any major occasion that includes a ceremonial ritual, such as a wedding, coming of age, or funer-al. A potlatch includes tribal dancing, tales of a family's sacred history, a feast, and the giving of gifts to the guests. Traditionally, the potlatch ceremony was a way of distributing wealth within the community. The more status and wealth a family had, the more it could, and did, give away. Hundreds of people were invited to a potlatch, and each guest received presents such as blankets, towels, kitchen utensils, and other practical items. In modern times, the potlatch is usually more modest, but people still dance, feast, and distribute gifts.

Some tribes hold their naming ceremonies twice a year. Tewa leaders create a sand painting and an altar and reenact the Tewa creation story. Mothers bring babies who have been born in the previous six months and make offerings of bread and flour. The tribal leaders receive the mothers one at a time and give the baby its name. The ceremony makes the child either a summer, or squash, person or a winter, or turquoise, person, a designation that he or she will keep throughout life and one that determines the role he or she will play in Tewa ceremonials.

The Power of Names

Names have the power to shape an individual's future. They are carefully chosen, often by an elder of the family or the tribe. Among some tribes, there is a belief that the souls of people who have died are reborn into the tribe, and children may receive their names. In other tribes, names may signify social rank or designate some characteristic that the namer hopes the child will have.

Girls usually keep their birth name throughout their lives, although among the Mandan, parents may hold a feast to rename a girl who is frail or unlucky, and thus give her a new start in life.

Boys may get new names at different times in their lives. A boy first gets a birth name, which he keeps through early childhood. As he matures, new responsibilities may be marked by his receiving a new name from tribal elders. Today both boys and girls commonly have both English and Indian names.

Childhood Rituals

Ceremonies for children often mark the roles they will take later in life or the qualities their parents wish them to have. They are aimed at ensuring such qualities as industry, strength, and courage. Tribal elders reinforce these qualities by telling children stories that stress them and by instructing them directly to be kind and responsible and to work hard.

The Navajo celebrate a baby's first laugh. Four days after the baby laughs for the first time, the baby's family invites family and friends from the larger community to join them for a large meal. The guests bring wishes for the child, traditionally wishing the opposite of what they hope for. They may, for example, wish that the child grow up to be ugly and selfish or sickly and bad tempered. By doing this, they are enlisting the spirits of their sacred clowns to help the baby through childhood. The guests all receive small gifts, such as coins, cookies, or kitchen items, as a symbol that the child will be generous and kind.

The giveaway ritual makes the child a full member of the tribe. After their first laugh, Navajo babies wear jewelry, such as bracelets or necklaces or buttons, as a token of their new status.

Traditionally, Native American children learn by watching and imitating their elders. Here, Suzie Yazzie demonstrates the art of Navajo weaving to her daughter.

The Lakota carry out a ritual in which families commit to bringing up their children according to Lakota values. A medicine woman pierces a girl's ears; a boy may have one ear pierced. The woman threads sinew, a narrow band of animal tissue, or a fine leather cord, into each hole so that it cannot close. The sinew symbolizes the traditional way of the Lakota, *Canku Luta,* the Pipe religion. An elder or a relative speaks to the children about the ceremony and what it means to be Lakota. Lakota children also take part in the *Hunkapi,* or "making of relatives" ceremony, where they hear about their sacred history and the words that Buffalo Calf Woman spoke to the children when she appeared to their people. After the ceremony, which may take place either separately or as part of the Sun Dance, families serve a ritual feast, and the child receives a new "spirit" name to mark his or her new, more grown-up status. The names are chosen by older relatives from the names of family members who have passed on. A *wihpeya,* or giveaway, completes the event. Customary gifts are towels, kitchen goods, cloth, and other useful items.

Between the ages of six and eight, Hopi children are believed to be old enough to understand the values underlying their religion and to begin to participate fully in the religious life of the community. They are taken to the *kiva,* or sacred dwelling, where for the first time they learn that the kachinas they have seen dancing are not spirits, but tribal members wearing costumes. Tribal elders explain that the costumed dancers personate Hopi deities and the values they represent. The ceremony inducts children into a kachina society and enables them to take part in Hopi rituals and ceremonies.

The Tewa conduct a Water Pouring ritual when a child is about ten years old. The child takes part in cleaning and preparing the kiva, which represents the place from which the Tewa people emerged according to their creation story. Children choose adults to be their sponsors and to instruct them in Tewa tribal knowledge. The children take gifts to their sponsors and do tasks that signify adulthood, boys by chopping wood and girls by grinding corn. The ceremony lasts four nights. On the final night, the children see masked dancers perform a Tewa ritual dance. Afterward, they have a ritual bath. The ceremony marks their passage to adulthood.

Puberty Rites

At one time, a girl's first menstrual period was a time marked by ceremony in almost all Native American tribes, because it signified that she was an adult and ready for marriage. As an adult woman, capable of bearing children, she had great creative power, equal to the power of the shaman to heal and give life. Power is, by itself, neither good nor bad, but it is always potentially dangerous. At puberty, a young woman had to learn the restrictions and taboos that went along with her new powers. Women were often isolated from the other members of the tribe during menstruation, forbidden to handle food or to touch other members of the tribe. In that way, these young women would not harm anyone accidentally.

Today, most tribes no longer celebrate a puberty rite for each girl who becomes a woman. Some tribes celebrate a coming-of-age ceremony once a year for the girls of the tribe who have reached puberty that year. Navajo and Apache still celebrate a girl's first menstrual period with a four-day ceremony and feast.

Apache Puberty Rites

Among the Apache, a shaman, who may be either a man or a woman, conducts the puberty ceremony that was handed down to the Apache by White Painted Woman, an important being in the tribe's sacred history. The ceremony includes feasting and dancers wearing costumes of the *gan,* Apache mountain spirits similar to Hopi kachinas and Navajo yei. The ceremony is lavish; there may be anywhere from four to sixteen dancers, plus one or two sacred clowns.

On the first day, family members put up a tipi with a framework of four spruce saplings. The young woman and a female attendant, usually the girl's aunt or grandmother, live there during the ceremony. The girl wears a special dress made of buckskin and painted yellow, the color of corn pollen. It symbolizes the costume worn by White Painted Woman. The dress is decorated with moon, sun, and star designs, and its fringe represents sunbeams.

■ *During her puberty ceremony, a young Apache woman and her sponsor await the blessing of an Apache shaman.*

At the close of the puberty ceremony, the young woman is blessed by being sprinkled with cattail pollen, which symbolizes life and fertility.

From her attendant, the young woman learns the many taboos she must observe. Her future depends on how she acts during the four days of the ceremony, which symbolizes the "pollen path," or the path of life that she will walk as an adult woman. If she becomes angry, in her future life she will be mean. If she is disobedient, she will bring bad weather. She must not smile or laugh, because if she does, her face will wrinkle. If she is pleasant and good-natured, however, she will be so all her life, and her life will be long, happy, and healthy.

The shaman who is conducting the ceremony sings while the young woman dances, for as long as six hours at a time, on a buckskin inside the tipi. Between sacred songs, her sponsor massages her body to shape and mold it so it will be strong. The young woman may rest between songs, but because puberty gives her special powers, including the power to cure, many sick people may visit her between songs so that she may touch them. At night, gan dancers, people wearing the costumes that represent mountain spirits, perform to drive away any evil spirits in the area. They, too, have the power to cure, and may be called on to heal between dances.

As the ceremony draws to a close, the shaman sprinkles the young woman's head with cattail pollen, a symbol of fertility and life. He also empties the contents of a small basket onto her head. It contains coins, corn kernels, and candy that represent the gifts that the family will give away. By this act, the family's gifts are sanctified. According to Apache belief, those who get candy will always have enough to eat; those who receive and plant the corn will have good harvests, and those who get coins will become wealthy.

The young woman dances in place while the guests greet her and ask her to use her power with White Painted Woman to grant their wishes. She then shakes out the buckskin and blankets used in the ceremony to symbolize that she will always have plenty of blankets and food and that her home will always be clean and tidy.

On the fourth day, the guests go home and the tipi is taken down. The family remain together until the ninth day, when the young woman is ritually bathed with suds from the yucca plant. After this ceremony, she is considered to be ready for marriage.

Navajo Puberty Rites

The Navajo observe a similar puberty rite patterned on the rituals first observed by Changing Woman. It is called *kinaalda*, and it is part of the Blessingway, the basic Navajo chant for harmony and balance. The Navajo believe that if the ritual is not observed, the girl may not come to realize the value of womanhood. Kinaalda lasts four days, symbolizing the length of time in which Changing Woman grew to womanhood. The Navajo puberty celebration is a series of endurance tests for the young woman. She runs so that she will be energetic and strong all her life, and she must not fall or look back because to do so will bring bad luck. Between racing and dancing, she works, usually at grinding corn. Again, her behavior at this time is thought to be an indication of how she will be as an adult. If she does not work hard, for example, she will be lazy all her life. On the final day, the ceremony lasts all night, and the young woman must stay awake so that the power that has come to her through the ceremony will not be interrupted, bringing bad luck.

Lakota Puberty Rites

Lakota girls traditionally stay with an older relative, an aunt or a grandmother, when they have their first menstrual

---

■ Navajo Puberty Rite Tradition

Rites of passage are often tied to a tribe's sacred history. The Navajo trace the girl's puberty rite to what the Holy People did for Changing Woman when she reached maturity. In the words of one elder,

"According to our legend, when Changing Woman had her first period they prepared her by using the dews of various plants. They put that into her body to enable her to produce offspring for the human race. On that account today we believe that when a girl has her first period...it is something sacred to us."

from *The Sacred: Ways of Knowledge, Sources of Life*, by Peggy Beck, Anna Lee Walters, and Nia Francisco. Navajo Community College Press, 1977, 1992.

period. While there, they are instructed in the meaning of womanhood and kept busy. The work they do has special meaning. Sewing and beading are symbols of caring for a family, quilting of thrift and hard work, preparing food of hospitality. Their sponsoring relative reminds them to avoid bad or angry thoughts, which might make them nasty or bad tempered for the rest of their lives.

During this time, the young woman is taught that all life is sacred. She is reminded to thank Wakan Tanka for the blessings of life and health and to pray in times of trouble or need. Prayers are offered that the young woman will be industrious and pure and will become a good woman, a good worker, and a good mother, one who treats guests with hospitality.

■ *Native American boys join their elders in ceremonies from an early age. Here, a boy of the Tohono O'odham waits his turn to perform in a dance.*

At the end of four days, the family traditionally holds a feast for their daughter and invites the entire community. Today this is usually done only for the oldest daughter in a family. Girls' coming of age may also be recognized as part of the Sun Dance or a Hunkapi ceremony, one of the seven sacred rites of the Lakota.

Boys' Coming of Age

Native American groups generally did not have a specific ceremony to mark a boy's transition into manhood. Boys received the privileges of adulthood as they earned them, for example, by mastering or demonstrating a skill such as hunting. The family of a boy who demonstrated that he was ready for new responsibilities might honor him with a feast, at which time he might receive a new name. On the Plains and in the Plateau regions, boys approaching puberty might go on their first vision quest or undergo fasting and other trials symbolic of entering into manhood.

Marriage

Native Americans have traditionally expected young people to marry and have children so that the tribe would continue and prosper. Families often took part in choosing mates for their children of marriageable age. Marriage ceremonies varied, but they usually included the giving of gifts, a feast, and dancing. Today most Native Americans are married in civil or church ceremonies to satisfy United States and Canadian laws. Couples may, however, choose to renew their marriage commitment with traditional tribal ceremonies.

A Hopi couple declare their intention to wed by sprinkling corn meal at dawn on the eastern edge of their village. To prepare for the wedding ritual, the bride to be moves in with the groom's family. By doing so, she demonstrates her commitment to nurturing her family and her people before the kachinas. At the groom's home she fasts and grinds corn for the family's use. During this time, the groom's relatives weave two robes and a sash for the bride. She will wear one robe and the sash at the wedding; the other will be saved for her burial.

On the wedding day, the bride dresses in her wedding robe and carries the second robe and several ears of corn wrapped in a reed mat. After prayers at the groom's home, she leads a procession to her parents' home. Behind her come the groom's family, carrying food and gifts. When the procession reaches the bride's home and the bride's family welcomes them, the ceremony is complete. In earlier times, the couple lived with the bride's family until they built their own house. Now they may simply return home.

Maturity

Midlife is a time when people become tribal leaders. It takes years to acquire the knowledge necessary to become a shaman or a leader in a medicine society, and it is not until midlife that people master it. Women, too, become shamans, or medicine women at midlife, when their childbearing years are over.

Older people are honored for their wisdom and knowledge. In the Northwest, people work hard for material success so that they can share it in a potlatch. Maturity is a time of giving back in a culture that prizes generosity. A long life is a blessing from the Great Spirit. People who attain old age are called on to give advice and pass on tribal lore to children, with whom they have a special relationship. Teaching children about their sacred history and culture is an important function for people in old age.

Death

Among most Native American peoples, death has always been accepted as a natural and inevitable part of the cycle of life. People expected their bodies to return to Mother Earth and their souls to move on to the next world, where they would live much as they had lived in this life. For this reason the dead of some tribes were buried with weapons, food, clothes, jewelry, and dishes that they might need in the next world. Chief Seattle, a nineteenth-century leader of the Suquamish people, expressed Native American belief this way: "There is no death. Only a change of worlds."

Funeral and mourning practices vary greatly from tribe to tribe. Many tribes compare death to a journey. The Ojibwa

> **■ Wintu Song for the Dead**
>
> Many tribes believed that the dead traveled to a place beyond the Milky Way, a land of beautiful flowers, tall forests, and rich pastures. This song expresses Wintu belief.
>
> *It is above that you and I shall go;*
> *Along the Milky way you and I shall go;*
> *along the flower trail you and I shall go;*
> *Picking flowers on our way you and I shall go.*
>
> from *Wintu Songs*, translated from the Wintu by D. Demetracopoulous, 1935.

buried their dead in a sitting position, facing west, the direction of the setting sun and the one in which they will travel. Items they need for the journey are buried with them—such things as moccasins, a blanket, a kettle, and materials to start a fire. Ojibwa dead are believed to travel on a deep path for four nights. They must cross a sinking bridge over rough waters, camp along the way in darkness, and pass through prairies before they come to the land of spirits, a beautiful place of clear lakes and streams, tall forests and grassy plains, where they are greeted with rejoicing and singing.

At Winnebago funerals, friends and family members address the spirit of the departed person. Usually the speakers explain the path that the spirit must take, and they ask that he or she not look back with longing at the lives of the living or linger around them, but move on to the world of spirits.

By tradition, the Navajo have always hated and feared death, which they believe happens when the wind of life that entered the body at birth departs. In Navajo belief, the good parts of the person's soul become part of the harmony and balance of the universe, but the bad parts remain behind. These evil influences walk the earth as ghosts and witches and have the power to harm the living.

The Navajo destroy the clothes and possessions of the dead person and are careful never to speak the person's name because to do so might attract his or her wandering ghost.

Today, many Native American groups interweave traditional and Christian ceremonies. After a death, they may hold a wake, a gathering of friends and family who sit with the body before burial, in the Christian tradition. But Native American traditions are also observed. People bring food for the funeral feast. Objects with sacred meaning for Native Americans, such as prayer pipes fetishes, or eagle feathers may be placed in the casket along with the body. Friends and family sit together and talk about the person who has died. Women may cry and wail as signs of mourning. Music may include both Christian hymns and Native American drumming and song.

After a funeral that is basically Christian, mourners may hold a funeral feast. In some traditions, such as Lakota, it was customary to give away all of the dead person's possessions so that the soul would not linger but set off promptly for the next world. A lavish feast and giveaway help to send the soul of the dead person on its way. A memorial feast a year later ends the official mourning period.

The Cycle of Life

From birth to death, Native Americans live with an awareness of their place in the universe and their relationship to the Great Spirit and the spirit world. There is no part of life that is not valuable. The vast number of rituals that mark the passages from one stage of life to another help to keep people on the path and to bind them to their family and their community.

CHAPTER 7

Native American Religions and Christianity

*T*he European explorers who came to America in the sixteenth and seventeenth centuries saw an "empty" land. It had no European-style buildings and cities, so to their way of thinking, it was "uninhabited" and ideal for colonization. The countries that claimed territories in the Americas knew that people already lived there, but they viewed these native people as "uncivilized," which to them meant non-European, and thus unimportant to them.

Native peoples, for their part, did not understand the European notion that land could be parceled out and owned. To them, the land they lived on, like the air they breathed, was a blessing from the Great Spirit. It was a living spirit. Who could own Mother Earth? The idea sounded as foolish as owning the rain or the sunshine. Only after they were driven off their ancestral lands by ever increasing numbers of immigrants did the idea sink in that the newcomers meant to take their land and keep it.

A Clash of Cultures

The countries that claimed land in America—England, France, and Spain—were overwhelmingly Christian. They intended to make the new land Christian as well.

In many ways, Christianity was the opposite of the native religions. For one thing, Christianity taught that the creatures and resources of the earth were given by God to humans to use as they saw fit. This notion bred the idea that the earth and the animals were much less important than humankind was. Native American beliefs tended to place humans on an equal footing with other creatures, with each having different, but not neces- sarily greater or lesser, gifts. Moreover, the Native American belief that the earth was alive and required reverence and respect was very different from the European notion that its bounty was there simply to be taken and used.

Another idea fostered by Western religions, Christianity included, was that their belief system was "true" and other reli- gions were "false." Those people who did not conform to Christian doctrines were "heathens" or "pagans." Not having been saved for eternity by faith in the one true religion, such people either counted for nothing or had to be converted, by force or by government order if necessary.

The explorer Christopher Columbus wrote in his journal that the native people he met had "as much lovingness as though they would give their hearts." Other explorers, too, noted that the people they met were extremely friendly—gener- ous and giving, trusting and kind. Many early explorers used Native American guides and sheltered with native tribes.

In their tradition of hospitality, Native Americans at first welcomed and tried to help European settlers, most of whom were often poorly equipped for survival in the new land. Many tribes took nonnatives into their families or adopted them as "blood brothers," making them honorary tribal members. Their generosity and trust gave way only gradually.

Colonization Begins

The Pilgrim settlers who came to Massachusetts from England in 1609 were seeking religious freedom, but they wanted it for themselves, not for others. They were highly intolerant of any beliefs that differed from theirs. They survived as a colony at least partly because of the help they received from the native people. The Wampanoags, under the legendary Massasoit, gave them seed corn and taught them how to plant it, saving them from starvation. But the acts of Massasoit's people did not stop the New England settlers from thinking of Native Americans as "savages."

As the colonies grew and European culture flourished in America, colonists' attitudes toward the Native Americans hardened. Overall, they tended to view the beliefs and ceremonies of native peoples as heathen superstitions and the people as being ripe for conversion to Christianity. From as early as 1617, the stated goal of white America was to "promote civilization among the savages." Missionaries were encouraged to work actively to convert the native peoples to Christianity.

The Missionary Effort

Close on the heels of the explorers came Roman Catholic priests to establish missions throughout North America and members of other religious groups to work among the native peoples. Their efforts to convert native peoples succeeded in some places and failed in others. Yet almost everywhere, Christianity had an effect on the native religions.

Southwestern Missions

As early as 1550, King Charles I of Spain (also known as Charles V of the Holy Roman Empire) called scholars together to discuss and determine how best to Christianize the Indians in the Americas. They reached the conclusion that the native people were slaves by nature, and they recommended a system called *encomienda*, which gave the colonists the right to force native people to work for nothing on Spanish lands and to make them pay taxes in the form of crops. Moreover, the colonists could use whatever acts of war and violence might be necessary to conquer and convert the native tribes.

Around 1598, Catholic missionaries settled among the Pueblo groups in the Southwest. Over the next forty years, they worked to convert the people. Mainly this meant using native people as forced labor to build chapels and mission buildings and compelling them under threat of whipping to be baptized, attend mass, and go to confession. The Spanish actively opposed Native American rituals. They raided the kivas, or religious chambers, of the Pueblo and destroyed ceremonial masks and other sacred objects. Some native spiritual leaders were hanged as witches. Colonists, including the priests, forced native people to work for them without compensation under the encomienda.

One effect of this Christian attempt to make converts in the Southwest was to drive native religious practice underground. While outwardly going along with the missionary program, the Pueblo peoples seethed with resentment and anger. They continued to practice their own religion in secret.

Popé and the Pueblo Revolt

In 1675, the Spanish governor, Juan Treviño, arrested forty-seven Pueblo medicine men and charged them with witchcraft. The Spanish whipped and tortured all and hanged several. Before they could kill the rest, a group of armed Pueblo forced the governor to release the remaining prisoners. One prisoner, a spiritual leader named Popé, began to plot to drive the Spanish out. By the summer of 1680, he had enlisted leaders from almost every surrounding village. The revolt began on August 9, 1680, and bloody fighting followed. In the end, the Pueblo were able to force the Spanish to withdraw completely.

Popé emerged as the leader of the Pueblo, and at his order, they destroyed the Christian churches and symbols. Christian marriages were declared invalid, and people returned to their traditional religious practices. The rebellion had a long-lasting effect. When Spanish missionaries returned after the death of Popé, they did not try to reinstate the encomienda or stamp out the Pueblo religions, which still survive.

The Mission of San Xavier del Bac

Some native groups did adopt Christianity. Spanish missionaries moved into what is now the Sonoran desert area in the late 1600s to work among the tribes who called themselves Tohono O'odham, "People of the Desert" (formerly known as Papago), and Pima. Like the Pueblo, the Tohono O'odham and

the Pima tried to resist the forced labor of and conversion by the Spanish. Unlike the Pueblo, however, they lost the fight, in 1751.

In the Pima settlement of Bac, which the Spanish renamed San Xavier del Bac, Franciscans ordered the construction of a spectacular mission church in Spanish cathedral style. The mission, built almost entirely by native laborers, was dedicated in 1797. Today it stands on the Papago Indian Reservation created by the United States government in 1874. The population of the reservation is and has been overwhelmingly Roman Catholic for more than two centuries.

The San Xavier Mission, dedicated in 1797, stands today on the Papago Indian Reservation near Tuscon, Arizona.

Other Missionary Efforts

The explorer-priest Jacques Marquette, a French Jesuit, began traveling through the upper Midwest, near the headlands of the Mississippi River, in 1666. Marquette, who established his first mission in 1675, by all accounts treated Native Americans fairly and with love and made many friends among them.

Another noted missionary effort—although a more brutal one—took place in California, where Father Junipero Serra set up the first of twenty-one missions in 1769. Serra's missions gave Spain a foothold in California. The system uprooted the local tribes, however, seized their lands, forced conversions, and exacted forced labor from the Indians. During this period (1769–1834) nearly half the Indian population died. From the beginning, Indians attempted to resist; most rebellions, however, were not successful.

The Iroquois

Jesuits (members of a Catholic religious order) moved into eastern Canada in the early 1600s and worked among the Iroquois. They were followed in the next century by Quaker missionaries. (Quakers were members of the Society of Friends, a religious sect that originated in England.) Notably, the Quakers did not try to convert the Iroquois to Christianity. They recognized in traditional Iroquois beliefs the same "inner light" of humanity that they themselves believed in. Certain Christian ideas did become part of the Iroquois belief system, however. For example, the Iroquois began to think of the Great Spirit as "the Creator," a deity with human form who cared about individuals and their welfare.

Another factor influencing the Iroquois not to convert to the Quakers' religion and to retain many of their traditional religious beliefs and traditions was a prophet named Handsome Lake (Skaniadariio). The half brother of Cornplanter, a chief of the Seneca, an Iroquois tribe, he had wasted his youth in drunkenness and wild living. In 1799, Handsome Lake had the first of several visions in which a messenger told him to give up his sinful ways and become a spiritual leader of his people.

Although he was influenced by Christian ideas, Handsome Lake preached a return to the traditional religion of the Iroquois—really, to his modified vision of the traditional religion, which now included some Christian concepts. He emphasized hard work, sobriety, and family. He encouraged people to accept the benefits of white society while keeping to their own Iroquois values and beliefs. Handsome Lake's "new road," established regular feasts: midwinter, strawberry time, and green corn harvest. His appeal was so powerful that even after his death, when a new missionary movement tried to convert the Iroquois to Christianity, his "Good Word" (*Gaiwiio*) endured. Eventually, Handsome Lake's teachings evolved into an Iroquois religious movement known as the Longhouse Religion, after the traditional building where meetings are held. This religion is still practiced among the Iroquois today.

Christianity and the Seminole

White settlement put native peoples under great social and religious pressures. The Seminole, originally members of the Creek tribe of Georgia, moved to Florida in the mid-1700s to get away from spreading European settlement. When white settlers began their move into Florida, the Seminole resisted and so gained a reputation for being troublesome. In the years 1817–18, General Andrew Jackson led his troops against the Seminole in the First Seminole War. At the time, Florida was Spanish territory; Jackson's invasions eventually led to Spain's turning over Florida to the United States.

Jackson became president of the United States in 1829, his reputation as a tough Indian fighter an important part of his image. Under Jackson, the Seminole, Cherokee, Creek, Choctaw, and Chickasaw tribes were relocated by forced march from their ancestral homes in the Southeast to land in Oklahoma in what is known as the "Trail of Tears." Forced to walk the great distance, many thousands of these people died.

Some Seminole fled into the Florida Everglades, where they continued to wage war against United States troops. In 1835, the Second Seminole War broke out. Under their leader Osceola, the Seminole fought cleverly and effectively. Even after Osceola was captured and died in prison, they continued to fight. The war finally wound down in 1842 without a decisive victory on either side and without surrender by the Seminole. Another effort to control and relocate the Seminole took place in 1855–58, but was

Native American converts to Christianity translated the words to familiar hymns into their own languages. Here are phonetic transcriptions of the Christian hymn "Amazing Grace" as sung by different tribes in the Oklahoma Missionary Conference.

Amazing grace! How sweet the sound
that saved a wretch like me!
I once was lost, but now am found;
was blind, but now I see.

Cherokee:
OOH NAY THLA NAH, HEE OO WAY GEE'.
E GAH GWOO YA HAY EE.
NAW GWOO JOE SAH, WE YOU LOW SAY
E GAH GWOO YAH HO NAH.

Kiowa:
DAW K'EE DA HA DAWTSAHY HE TSOW'HAW
DAW K'EE DA HA DAWTSAHY HEE.
BAY DAWTSAHY TAW, GAW AYM OW THAH T'AW
DAW K'EE DA HA DAWTSAHY H'EE

Creek:
PO YA FEK CHA HE THLAT AH TET
AH NON AH CHA PA KAS
CHA FEE KEE O FUNNAN LA KUS
UM E HA TA LA YUS.

Choctaw:
SHILOMBISH HOLITOPA MA!
ISHMMINTI PULLA CHA
HATAK ILBUSHA PIA HA
IS PI YUKPALASHKE.

from *The United Methodist Hymnal*, Nashville, Tenn.: The United Methodist Publishing House, 1989.

also unsuccessful. Descendants of this Seminole band live in Florida to this day.

Baptist missionaries, preaching in the Seminole language, began working to convert the people as they arrived on the Oklahoma reservation. The two religions blended, as Christian traditions worked their way into Seminole rituals and vice versa. Stomp Dance songs took on the character of Christian gospel music, led by a singer who sang each line for people to follow. Christian churches developed hymns in the Seminole language with Native American tunes. Seminole Baptist churches featured fasting and spontaneous prayer and preaching, holdovers from Seminole rites. As people adapted to their new surroundings, they identified new places as sacred and would sometimes withdraw to them to seek a vision or the answer to a problem from the Christian God.

The Seminole who remained in Florida met Christianity in the early 1900s when converts from their own tribe began to preach to them in their own language. A sizable portion of the tribe converted, rejecting traditional Seminole ritual and belief. The Seminole Christians refused to participate in rituals such as the Green Corn Dance, the world renewal ceremony that had been at the center of Seminole culture. Although traditional practices continued among the people who had not converted, religious differences weakened tribal bonds.

The Reservation System

During the 1800s, many other tribes were forced onto reservations, often thousands of miles from their ancestral homes. These reservations were frequently located on land no one else wanted. Agricultural tribes found themselves on barren, dry plains where nothing would grow, and hunting tribes found themselves on land where little, if any, game were available. People were separated from their sacred sites. Reservations became places of unemployment, poverty, and alcoholism, places where people lived in great despair.

Tribes like the Navajo and Hopi, parts of whose ancestral lands were designated as reservations, fared better. Because they remained close to their sacred sites, they were able to maintain their traditional culture and religion to a large degree. However, these places, too, suffered economically.

Bans on Native Religious Practice

By the mid-1800s, there were few places left in America that Native Americans could go to escape the spread of white culture. In the 1700s, settlement in the East had forced them onto the Plains. When the railroad cut through the Plains, that place, too, was no longer a haven.

Contact with white America threw Native American society into cultural and religious conflict. Pressures to conform to modern ways led people away from traditional beliefs, toward acceptance of Christianity. Native Americans began, like the white society around them, to separate the sacred from the secular, something they had never done before.

When Native Americans were forced off their ancestral lands and moved onto reservations, they came under government control. The United States Bureau of Indian Affairs put white appointees, known as Indian agents, in charge of administering tribal business. These agents made regulations that were often enacted into law by the federal government. The Courts of Indian Offenses, established in 1883, banned "old heathenish dances." It also barred medicine men from performing rituals and ordered an end to some mourning practices, such as the destruction of property. Its rulings remained in place until 1934.

The Sun Dance became illegal, along with other feasts and dances. The Sun Dance had been central to the cultural and religious life of the Plains tribes. They searched for ways to continue it. They dropped aspects that the white officials objected to and presented it as a cultural festival rather than a religious ceremony. The Shoshone added Christian symbolism. Somewhat changed in character, the dance continued.

In Canada, from 1876 to 1951, it was illegal for Native Americans to practice their religious rites. On the Northwest Coast, Native Americans did manage to conduct some ceremonies in secret; others they changed to make them more acceptable to white authorities. The potlatch ceremony, for example, became more of a secular giveaway than a religious ceremony.

Many Northwest Indians became Christian during this time. The difficulties of maintaining traditional ways led many people to abandon ancestral religions. In the seventy-five years of the ban, some traditions were lost as spiritual leaders died without passing on their knowledge.

John Slocum and the Indian Shaker Church

In the late 1800s, a religious leader, John Slocum, emerged in the Northwest. He was a member of the Squaxin, a Salish band of Puget Sound in Washington State. In 1881, when Slocum was about forty years old, a logging accident apparently took his life. His body was prepared for burial and the mourners gathered. Suddenly, he sat up and began to speak. Slocum told the astonished group that he had indeed died and had gone to the Christian heaven, where he saw a great light. An angel had sent him back with a message. People were to give up the practice of shamanism. They must avoid sins like smoking, gambling, and drinking and must pray regularly.

Slocum's followers built him a church in which he preached a basically Christian message. Slocum was influenced by Roman Catholicism, and he used aspects of Christian symbolism, such as a steeple, a cross, and hand-bell ringing. But the church had echoes of traditional Native American ritual as well. The preacher muttered words to an interpreter to be spoken aloud to listeners in the way of a shaman. The service was followed by a ceremonial feast in which people sat by their rank in the tribe, as at a potlatch.

About a year later, Slocum became ill and again appeared to die. His wife Mary called for his body be brought back to their house. She began to tremble violently and to pray aloud to Jesus, and Slocum began to show signs of life. After his recovery, he, too, adopted the custom of trembling or "shaking," believing it to be a sign of the great medicine power promised by the angel he had seen in his earlier vision.

Slocum's message was attractive to native people because it came from the direct experience of another Native American. His Indian Shaker Church, as it was named, gained many followers. It spread throughout the Northwest and into California. Local Protestant missionaries opposed it. They had Slocum jailed and forced him to attend Presbyterian services. The opposition ended, however, in 1892, when the Indian Shakers organized legally. The Indian Shaker Church took on many of the roles of the shaman, such as curing and finding lost objects, but members professed belief in God and Jesus, not the spirit world. Although small, the church still survives and still attracts converts, often people who come to be cured of illness through the power of prayer.

Indian Schools

The United States government mandated formal education for the Native American young people. Children, always considered the hope and future of a tribe, had always learned their skills and cultural traditions one-on-one from their elders, by watching and being included. Now, Christian missionaries were moving onto the reservations and establishing churches and schools. As young people reached school age, they were shipped off to boarding schools, often hundreds of miles from their homes, too distant for families to visit. In the summers, they were often sent to work for non-Indian families so they would be immersed in the life of the "white man." Schools such the Chilocco Indian School of Oklahoma, founded in 1884, and the Carlisle Indian School of Pennsylvania, founded in 1887, taught classes in English, and students were punished for speaking their native language. The schools banned native traditions and presented Christian beliefs instead.

By the time the young people graduated and returned to their homes on the reservation, many had lost their language and culture. Taught to believe that their own traditions were backward and superstitious, and resenting the Christian beliefs that had been forced on them, they felt lost in both worlds. Meanwhile, the spiritual leaders of an earlier generation were dying out. The young people to whom they should have been passing sacred knowledge no longer spoke their language. It was a bleak time for native religions.

The Ghost Dance

The Northern Paiute, or, in their own language, the Numu, "the People," of the Walker River area in Nevada, suffered enormously though the middle of the nineteenth century. Miners on their way to the California gold rush (1849) cut through their lands, destroying farmland and killing game. Then homesteaders moved in, taking the best land for themselves. The Numu fought back, but federal troops moved in and an uneasy truce began. A long drought brought hunger and the diseases of the white man, to which the Indians had no natural immunity, causing many of them to die.

On New Year's Day 1889, a Northern Paiute named
Wovoka had a vision. In it, a messenger from God told him to
preach that Indians and white people must be at peace. He also
received special powers, including the gift of predicting weather and making rain, and was told to introduce the Ghost Dance,
a round dance for spiritual renewal, in which people held hands
and moved in a circle, singing holy songs. During the dance,
people often saw visions of dead relatives returning.

Wovoka was a shaman's son and had probably learned
shamanistic skills from his father. As a child, he had heard the
prophesies of Wodziwob, an earlier Numu prophet who had
foreseen a time when the dead Native Americans would arise,
the buffalo would return, and white people would be gone. In
addition, Wovoka had grown up with white companions. At
their home, he had listened to stories from the Christian Bible.
All of these elements combined to make Wovoka one of the great
spiritual leaders of Native America.

News of Wovoka's vision spread. The Ghost Dance movement crossed tribal lines and united people who had remained separate for centuries. Among the Lakota, bitter about the loss of their lands to white interests, years of bloody warfare with federal troops, and a string of broken governmental promises, the Ghost Dance evolved to fit their needs. It became more warlike. One feature of the dance among the Lakota was the Ghost Shirt, a buckskin garment decorated with symbols that was believed to protect the wearer from bullets.

United States government agents viewed the Ghost Dance with alarm. They placed an absolute ban on its performance. At that time, they were then repressing all native rituals, but the Ghost Dance made them particularly nervous. Soldiers believed that it was a war dance, meant to whip the dancers into a frenzy for battle. Rumors that a Ghost Dance was going to be held led to an order for the tribal police to arrest Sitting Bull, a Lakota chief and spiritual leader. As he was seized, fighting broke out, and he was killed, along with eleven others.

Tribal leaders had never wanted to get into a battle with the United States. Sitting Bull's death frightened them. Another leader, Chief Big Foot, set out to lead his people to the Pine Ridge Reservation in North Dakota, where he felt they would be safe. But before they could get there, they were surrounded by U. S. Army troops and forced to camp at Wounded Knee Creek, where the soldiers trained machine guns on them. One of the leaders prayed aloud that the men's Ghost Shirts would protect them. Skirmishes broke out, and then the shooting began in earnest. The soldiers killed more than one hundred fifty men, women, and children in what came to be known as the Wounded Knee Massacre. Wovoka, in mourning, ordered that the Ghost Dances stop. For the most part, the Ghost Dance religion ended, although some small groups continued to practice it into the twentieth century.

The Native American Church

The Ghost Dance of 1890 had appealed to Native Americans of many different tribes. For the first time, they had begun to think of themselves less as members of individual tribes and more as "Native Americans." Politically, members of different tribes joined together in what was called the pan-Indian movement, which welcomed Native Americans of all tribal backgrounds. In the early twentieth century, an organization called the Native American Church was developed by those who practiced the peyote ritual, filling the gap left when the Ghost Dance died out. It blends native beliefs with aspects of Christianity.

A controversial aspect of the Native American Church has been the use of peyote, the fruit of a southwestern cactus that is a mild hallucinogen, or drug that alters consciousness. It was said that eating a small quantity of peyote may help people to have "visions" or cause them to see colored lights around objects. Native American Church members compare their use of peyote to the use of sacramental wine in Christian communion.

Peyote has been a part of Native American ritual for more than ten thousand years. An ancient Kiowa tale tells of a woman who was about to give birth. Traveling with her people across the desert, she fell behind and bore her child alone in the desert. She was ready to give up in despair when the spirit of the peyote came to her and told her to eat some of the plant. The peyote spirit gave her strength and led her home. She taught the people the spirit's prayers and songs and began the peyote tradition, and she is honored as Peyote Woman.

Bans on the use of peyote go back to 1620, when the Spanish declared its use to be heresy. By the end of the nineteenth century, Christian missionaries and Indian agents called peyote use a "heathen superstition" that had to be replaced by Christianity. In 1888, the Indian agent of the Kiowa, Comanche, and Wichita tribes banned its use in religious ceremonies. Two years later, the ban was adopted by the United States government. Government agents raided peyote ceremonies. They arrested worshipers, who were sent to jail or fined, and seized property on which the ceremony was conducted.

Acts of Congress passed in 1965 and 1970 allowed the use of peyote for religious purposes, but arrests continued. Some federal officials still seized peyote even after the American Indian Religious Freedom Act of 1978 specifically permitted its use.

The Peyote Ritual

There are two versions of the basic peyote ritual: the Half-Moon Ceremony (Tipi Way) and the Quanah Parker, or Kiowa, Way. Both are similar, however. The peyote ritual takes place around a crescent- or horseshoe-shaped earthen altar. The ritual leader, called the roadman, holds a feathered staff and a rattle. He is assisted by the chief drummer, who beats the water drum; cedarman, who holds a bag of cedar needles; and fireman, who makes and tends the fire, which has four logs pointing in the four directions of the compass. The leader passes the peyote around the circle along with the rattle, and each participant takes some of the peyote and sings.

During the ceremony, those taking part may see spirits or angels or may receive instructions on how to live a better life. They call on the peyote spirit, whom they see as one with God, Christ, and the Great Spirit. The ceremony cleanses the participants of evil influences. At the end, a woman who symbolizes Peyote Woman brings water to the participants, and they refresh themselves. Afterward, people come to be healed and to testify about how the religion has made them better people. The peyote road, as it is called, demands high moral standards. People must not drink, gamble, or quarrel, must work hard, and must treat their families with love and respect.

Peyotism filled a need that many Native Americans felt for a religion of their own not dominated by white America. In 1944, it was incorporated as the Native American Church of the United States; five years later it changed its name to the Native American Church of North America to include Canadians. While information is somewhat elusive, recent estimates give the number of followers as 100,000 to 225,000. It is incorporated in seventeen states but is still the religion of only a small minority of Native Americans. Some tribes have no adherents.

Christianity and Native Religions

Contact with Christian European-Americans meant great challenge and change for Native Americans. From the first, many Native American spiritual leaders recognized in the Christian God similarities to the Great Spirit that they had

worshipped from the beginning of time. The European settlers who colonized North America, however, for the most part rejected any such relationship. Missionary efforts and government policies directly assaulted Native American religions as European settlement assaulted their culture.

Native Americans met the challenge in different ways. Many embraced Christianity. Others adapted and incorporated aspects of it into their own belief systems. Christian thought influenced a number of religious movements, including The Iroquois Longhouse Religion, the Indian Shaker Church, the Ghost Dance Religion, and the Native American Church, that remain distinctively Native American.

In spite of four hundred years of strong efforts to stamp out Native American religions, a number of them, particularly in the American Southwest and the Plains but in other parts of North America as well, have continued into the present. Their survival demonstrates the strength and vitality of Native American religious belief.

■ *Quanah Parker, son of a Comanche chief and a white woman captured as a child by the Comanche, became both a highly respected chief of his people and a successful businessman. A roadman (leader) in the peyote religion, he attracted many followers to peyotism and battled the U.S. government for the right to practice it.*

CHAPTER 8

Native American Religions Today

*T*he late twentieth century has brought a renewal of interest in native cultures, particularly on the reservations and among people of Indian descent. More people are identifying themselves as Native Americans. Young people are trying to learn more about their heritage, taking an active part in dances and attending events such as powwows, gatherings that bring different tribes together.

Non-Indians, too, are learning more about native cultures and religions. Works by Native American artists and craftspeople are in demand. Groups such as the American Indian Dance Theater carry Native American culture to a wide audience.

Native American religions have benefited from this renewed interest. Religious practices that had almost died out have been revived. On the Canadian Northwest Coast, where the ban on religious practices ended in 1951, people are once again gathering for potlatches, although some ritual practices have been lost. In the United States, ceremonies such as the Sun Dance, which had become more of a cultural event in the early part of the century, have begun a return to their religious center.

Spiritual leaders are practicing ceremonies for curing more freely, and more people are participating.

Native American Religions and Modern Society

In the past, native religions succeeded largely because they were the product of small, tightly knit communities. People lived together. They knew each other and took responsibility for each other as brothers and sisters. When Native Americans moved to the cities, community values naturally became more difficult, if not impossible, to hold on to. Besides, people in cities tend to be cut off from their relationship with the land, which is an essential part of native worship.

From the time the United States government forced them onto reservations, Native Americans—with good reason—resented government interference in their lives. For many native religions, however, the reservation system has proved to be a saving factor. People on the reservations have the advantage of being part of a close-knit community, connected by their ancient heritage and their customs and having similar goals. They have been able to preserve their religious customs and to pass them on to the next generation.

Many Native Americans today have grown up as Christians. Their families converted during the time when it was against the law to practice traditional religions. Even practicing Native American Christians, however, may participate in healing or other ceremonies that bring them closer to their cultural heritage. They see no conflict, believing as their ancestors did that the Christian God and the Great Spirit are both expressions of the same Power.

Changing Times

The 1970s were a time of political change and protest in the United States and Canada. People became much more aware of their civil rights. Many people began to take pride in their racial and ethnic backgrounds. Native Americans were no exception. They publicly challenged the stereotypes that they felt harmed and demeaned them and the government policies that they found objectionable.

The formation of AIM (American Indian Movement) led to clashes between protesters and the U.S. government, and several people died. This extreme phase of the movement did not last long, but it sparked new awareness. Native Americans in both the United States and Canada began to think about how they could use political means to improve their situation.

Tribal councils became more active in negotiating with the government. The Indian nations in the United States already had constitutions and political structures similar to those outlined in the U.S. Constitution, and the United States recognized them as separate nations within U.S. boundaries. Native Americans found that they could use these tools to govern themselves and to ensure their rights. In recent years, as tribal leaders have taken more control within the reservation, they have learned to make the reservation system work for them. They have taken advantage of their status as independent nations to write business contracts that are favorable to them.

Self-government is also an issue in Canada, where political and economic opportunities for native peoples have been even slower to arrive than in the United States. An encounter between the Mohawk and the Canadian Army in 1990 led to a government study of Canadian policies regarding its native peoples. The study report, released in 1996, made more than four hundred recommendations for improving the relationship between Canada and its Indians and Inuit. These included recognition of the Indian bands that live in Canada's 633 reservations as sovereign nations empowered to govern themselves without undue government interference. Many of these reservation areas are tiny, however, perhaps only the size of a village, so real political power remains beyond their grasp.

Canadian tribes, like their United States counterparts, have used existing laws to file claims in every province on land that they believe was wrongfully taken from them. Where land has been returned to Canadian tribes, those tribes have demonstrated an ability to manage it successfully. The Inuk people of northern Quebec, who received territory in a 1975 settlement, now own three local airlines and are building several factories to process caribou meat.

Native Americans and the Environmental Movement

Environmentalism, another political movement of the 1970s, led Americans to take a serious look at the way they were using, or misusing, their natural resources. A natural alliance sprang up between some Native American spiritual leaders and those environmentalists who were interested in protecting the earth on which they lived and its resources. Environmentalists often hold up Native American beliefs about the sacredness of the environment as the standard for which modern society should be striving. American Indian philosophy regarding conservation and the land is better known and more widely respected today than it was only a few decades ago, and many non-Indians have adopted Native American attitudes toward the natural world and ecological soundness.

Gaining Religious Freedom

For Native Americans in the United States, achieving religious freedom has been a long process. It took them two hundred years to win the right to religious freedom guaranteed two hundred years earlier to other Americans by the Bill of Rights, the first ten amendments to the U.S. Constitution. Although their right to freedom of religion had been recognized by the courts as early as 1934, when bans on their dances and other religious practices were lifted, Native American religions were not legally protected until President Jimmy Carter signed the American Indian Religious Freedom Act (AIRFA) of 1978. Even then, problems remained. When Native Americans tried to use AIRFA in court, they found that it was often not specific enough to be of much help.

The use of peyote by the Native American Church has come under attack. In 1990, the Supreme Court found that the state of Oregon could ban the use of peyote for religious purposes as a dangerous drug. Only under the Religious Freedom Restoration Act of 1993 and the American Indian Religious Freedom Amendment of 1994, signed by President Bill Clinton, have Native American religious practices become fully protected.

The Canadian Indian Act of 1885 had made participating in a potlatch a crime, drastically harming religious practices of many Canadian tribes of the Northwest Coast. It was finally repealed in 1951, but for many tribes, the damage was already done. Many parents, having suffered through the bans on their language and their traditions, chose not to pass on their knowledge to their children, who often did not find out that they were Native American until they were in their teens. Only in recent years have these people, now adults, begun to explore their heritage. In some cases, this has meant inventing new customs along traditional lines, since the old ones have been lost.

Native American Religions and Popular Culture

Native American thought and belief have gained the attention of many non-Indians searching for spiritual meaning. In the minds of some Native Americans, however, popularity is in itself a problem. They point out that their religion is a way of life, a habit of thought acquired over a lifetime. It is not something that can be picked up in a class or from reading a book.

For people who are not well informed, telling the difference between a true spiritual healer and a fraud can be difficult. Traditional spiritual leaders scorn individuals who try to trade on Native American spirituality by calling themselves healers and claiming to pass on ancient secrets. Also, old stereotypes are hard to erase. Bookstores may still classify Native American religions as "new age" or popular psychology, rather than putting them in the religion section. This labeling reflects a continuing belief that somehow they are not "true" religions.

Some spiritual leaders do work with non-Indians, including them in rituals for renewal and healing. Among themselves, however, Native Americans have not fully resolved questions of whether their practice of religion should include outsiders or not. Many believe that the holiest of rituals should belong only to tribal members.

Continuing Tensions

Cultural differences between the governments of the United States and Canada the Native American tribes they administer still create tensions. Besides conflicts over fishing, hunting, and property rights, many of these problems have religious roots. They concern ceremonial space, sacred objects, and beliefs about life and death.

Sacred Land

Probably the most stubborn problem for Native Americans has been the question of land. The government and the courts have not always understood the concept of sacred land. For Native American worship, it is not enough to protect a sacred spring or rock, for example, by roping it off or fencing it in, as one might a church or a shrine. Its sacredness comes in part from its remoteness, its distance from the things of the world. Hiking trails and parking lots, even a mile or two away, which local authorities might consider a convenience, are a desecration to Native Americans.

Even Native Americans who live on or near reservations may be denied access to their sacred places, many of which exist on government property. And once sacred land is lost, getting it back can be a long struggle—or impossible.

■ *The Devil's Tower is located on the Belle Fourche River west of Black Hills, Wyoming. It is a sacred Indian site.*

The sacred history of the Taos people identifies Blue Lake as the place from which their people emerged at the beginning of time, and the place to which their souls go after death. In 1906, President Theodore Roosevelt signed an order making Blue Lake part of the Carson National Forest. The Taos people began trying to get their sacred place back immediately. Sixty-five years later, in 1970, President Richard Nixon finally signed an order returning it to them.

The sixty-five year struggle of the Taos people against the U.S. government had a positive outcome. But many other places, equally sacred, remain in government hands, and worshipers' access to them is restricted or denied. The governments of the United States and Canada have often argued that their right to dam, mine, or otherwise use lands outweighs Native American rights to those lands. United States courts, right up to the Supreme Court, have not been supportive of Native Americans in this regard, often viewing their claims as being about land rather than about worship. They have permitted such projects as the development of a ski area in the San Francisco Peaks, sacred to the Hopi and the Navajo, and the flooding of sacred Cherokee sites in the Tennessee Valley.

Setting aside dwindling wilderness lands with their potential water, lumber, mineral, and recreational value as sacred places has not proved popular. This conflict is likely to grow worse as wilderness declines. It is already difficult for people whose religions include vision quests to find a place sufficiently natural and isolated, a place where there are no jet planes passing overhead and no roads, hikers, loggers, or mountain bikers. Still, Native Americans themselves find the lessening of religious restrictions and the renewal of Native American rituals to be a hopeful sign.

Respecting Indian Ancestors

Anthropologists and archaeologists who study ancient cultures learn about them by uncovering the ruins of old villages and digging up burial sites. In the past, they took many things back to museums for study. In addition to artifacts such as weapons, jewelry, and cooking utensils, they often took human skeletons.

For many Native American groups, land in which tribal members are buried is sacred, and the burials themselves are sacred places. The dead are their ancestors, part of the unbroken chain of life that goes back to creation. In order for the tribe to be strong, the dead must rest in peace. The idea that the bones of thousands of their ancestors might be lying in museum laboratories—or worse, exhibited to museum-goers—was a long-time source of distress.

The Native American Graves Protection and Repatriation Act of 1990 (NAGPRA) gives Indian tribes control over any burial items or human skeletons found on federal and tribal lands. This act also provides that museums and other institutions that have such items in their collections return them for reburial if the tribes from whose land they came request it. Many tribes have successfully sued for the return of human remains found on their lands over the past hundred years. The law does not completely bar digging in burial sites, but it does help to reduce the chances that Indian graves will be desecrated.

For their part, archaeologists and anthropologists argue that if they are not allowed to examine and test human skeletons, much valuable information about Native Americans will be lost. One of the things scientists hope to learn more about is where these peoples came from in prehistory. Although some Native Americans agree with the goals of these scientists, others argue that they already know where they came from: they emerged or were created on this continent and they have no need to know more. The debate continues.

Protecting Sacred Objects

Laws to protect Native American sacred sites, objects, remains, and practices seem to be working, at least part of the time. In the 1970s, many sacred objects, such as medicine bundles, medicine masks, and fetishes (the small carved figurines that have medicine power) made their way into museums where they were displayed as curiosities. Native Americans felt these displays were an insult to their spiritual beliefs.

Today, under NAGPRA, many tribes are regaining possession of their sacred objects. A case in point is the return of Zuni

Twin War God fetishes. The Zuni place two of these wooden figures in a sacred shrine each year as their spiritual guardians. These War God fetishes have great power to cause natural disasters as well as wars and other tragedies if the people do not pray to them regularly.

Over the years, many War God fetishes disappeared from their shrines and turned up in museums. The Zuni successfully claimed that any figures that were not in their shrines had been stolen and must be returned. More than eighty of these figures have been returned, and the Zuni are continuing their efforts to find others, both in museums and in private collections around the world. Meanwhile, other groups have been studying the Zuni example to find out how to use federal laws to regain their own sacred objects.

The Eagle

To more than two hundred Native American tribes, the eagle is the spirit messenger that carries messages between the Great Spirit and the earth. Ceremonies performed with eagle feathers are at the heart of their religion. Eagle feathers are used in many kinds of rites, including curing rituals, world renewal ceremonies, and death rites.

To the U. S. government, the eagle is an officially threatened species, protected by law. Killing an eagle is a crime and, since the law presumes that anyone who has eagle feathers got them by harming an eagle, so is possessing and selling the feathers. In recent years, the government has made an effort to accommodate Native American religious needs, however. The government maintains the National Eagle Repository, which keeps all the eagles that are found dead in the United States. Native Americans who need an eagle or a number of eagle feathers can fill out a Native American Religious Purposes Permit application and receive an eagle if one is available.

This solution is not very satisfactory to many Native Americans, who ask how Christians would feel if they had to fill out a government application to get a Bible. Often there is a long wait, although the eagle repository tries to satisfy urgent requests immediately. But the fact that the government and the tribes are working together to find solutions that support native religious practices is a positive step.

The Challenge to Native Religions

From their first contact with Europeans up to the present, native peoples have had to struggle with outside influences that attempted to stamp out their religions. Their ceremonies have been banned and their sacred places taken from them. Their challenge has been to find a way to be true to their own traditions while living within white society. Somehow, their religions have managed to survive. Today, although much has been lost, Native American religious practices remain alive and strong.

Native American religions have roots that go back tens of thousands of years into prehistory. They are an unending path, like the path of life itself. Native people who follow that path understand that the world is not just a physical place. It is a spiritual universe, filled with sacredness and spirit power, one in which they walk daily and which guides their lives.

GLOSSARY

Blessingway—A Navajo ritual for restoring harmony to the earth, conducted both separately and as segment of healing rituals.

Buffalo Calf Woman—A representative of the Buffalo People, messengers of the Great Spirit, who brought the sacred pipe to the Lakota so that they might use it to do only good things—make peace between warring nations and to heal the sick.

Canku Luta—Lakota Pipe religion.

Changing Woman—Heavenly being to whom the Navajo trace their origins, who created corn and made the earth people; mother of twin sons, who lived with their father, the sun, who gave them special knowledge and powerful weapons for doing good.

Chantways—Navajo rituals for creating balance and harmony or for healing, lasting from one to nine days.

Coyote—A half-animal, half-human being who appears in the tales of many cultures as a trickster/creator.

Culture Hero—A supernatural being with creative powers, having human or animal form, who created the world, made it ready for humans, and taught the First People how to live on the earth.

Diyin Diné—Navajo Holy People, including First Man and First Woman, who emerged from a succession of underworlds to prepare the earth for humankind.

Emergence Tales—Sacred stories in which people are not created but emerge from the underworld or some other place, such as the bottom of a lake or a clamshell.

Encomienda—A sixteenth-century system under which Spanish colonists forced native people to work for nothing and to pay them taxes.

Gan—Apache mountain spirits similar to Hopi kachinas and Navajo yei.

Ghost Shirt—A buckskin garment, decorated with symbols, believed to protect the wearer from bullets.

Great Mystery—The Great Spirit; the Power underlying all creation.

Green Corn Dance—A ceremony shared by many agricultural peoples to give thanks to the creator for the year's bounty, and to pray for rain, the well-being of the people, and bountiful harvests.

Guardian Spirits—Spirit helpers, usually acquired in a dream or vision, that help shamans and other individuals contact higher powers.

Ha'athali—Navajo holy person or singer.

Hozho—(Navajo) harmony, a state of being in balance with the forces of nature.

Hunkapi—(Lakota) "making of relatives" ceremony.

Inikagapi—(Lakota) the Sweat Lodge Ceremony.

Kachina—An ancestral spirit venerated by some southwestern tribes and represented by costumes and masks with symbols of earth, sky, atmosphere, plants, and animals; a carved representation of a particular spirit

Koshare and Kurena—Pueblo spirit beings who taught the people how to make crops grow.

Kiva—Sacred ceremonial chamber of the Hopi and other southwestern tribes.

Manitou—(Algonquin) Great Spirit or Great Mystery.

Medicine Bundle—A collection of objects with sacred significance and spirit power, wrapped in an animal skin or in cloth. Medicine bundles are considered to be holy, living things.

Medicine Lodge—A sacred building, representing the universe, in which rituals are conducted by the Algonquin.

Medicine Man/Woman—A shaman, someone with special connections to the spiritual world and special powers, such as curing or fortelling the future.

Medicine Society—In northeastern tribes, an organization of people who pass through levels of mastery to learn tribal lore, healing rituals, sacred songs, and other sacred knowledge.

Mitakuye' Oyasin—(Lakota) A phrase meaning "All of creation are my relatives," traditionally spoken during a healing ceremony.

Object Intrusion—A cause of illness in which a foreign object, such as a stone or a bone, is believed to have entered a person's body.

Orenda—(Iroquois) the Great Spirit or Great Mystery.

Paho—Prayer sticks made by the Pueblo and left in sacred places to convey prayers to the spirit world.

Personate—To represent in material form the spirit whose costume or mask a sacred dancer wears, thus allowing that spirit to enter into the body of the dancer and link the human and supernatural worlds.

Peyote—Fruit of a southwestern cactus; a mild hallucinogen, or drug that alters consciousness, used ritually by members of the Native American Church.

Poeh—(Tewa) the path of life walked by the first ancestors.

Potlatch—A ceremonial feast and giveaway held by Northwest Coast tribes to celebrate any major occasion that includes a ceremonial rite, such as a wedding.

Puberty Rite—A ritual celebrating a girl's reaching womanhood.

Sacred Clowns—Dancers who, by their clownlike antics, represent the foolishness of humankind and provoke amusement and laughter during sacred dances.

Shaman—A person with a special calling that enables him or her to contact the spirit world for healing and other spiritual purposes. Also called medicine man or medicine woman, singer, and other names.

Singer—Navajo name for a holy person or religious leader.

Sky Woman—Heavenly being to whom the Iroquois and neighboring tribes trace their origins; mother of twin sons, who are considered the creators of the world as humans know it.

Soul Loss—A cause of illness in which evil spirits capture a sick person's soul and carry it to the underworld.

Spirit—The life, or breath, in all natural things, including sky-beings: sun, moon, and stars; spirits of the atmosphere: rain and wind; animal and plant spirits; powers of the underworld; and the spirits of the dead.

Sun Dance—A complex of rituals and dances performed by Plains tribes for world renewal, usually performed over four days.

Sweat Lodge Ceremony—A form of ritual purification that precedes all important ceremonies and is conducted separately for health and healing, practiced widely by Native Americans.

Taboo—A forbidden act; breaking a taboo can cause misfortune to an individual or a tribe.

Tijus-keha—Iroquois culture hero, Master of Life, son of Sky Woman, and twin to Tawis-karong, whose creations were evil.

Trickster—A supernatural being who plays practical jokes, breaks taboos, spoils the works of the culture hero, or otherwise makes trouble.

Vision Quest—A period of fasting, prayer, and isolation in a sacred place, during which a person may acquire a guardian spirit or spiritual guidance.

Wakan Tanka—(Lakota) the Great Spirit or Great Mystery.

Wapiye' Win—(Lakota) a medicine woman or "spirit-calling woman."

Water Pouring Rite—Tewa ritual conducted when a child is about ten years old to mark his/her passage into adulthood.

World Renewal—Ceremonies performed annually for maintaining order and harmony in the world.

Yei—A symbolic figure of the holy people who represent the higher forces of the Navajo universe.

CHAPTER NOTES

page 53   "I may pray with my mouth...." Red Weasel, in *A Cry from the Earth Music of the North American Indians*, by John Bierhorst, Santa Fe: Ancient City Press, 1979, p. 44.

page 77   "A miracle can happen..." (*See* For Further Reading, Corbin Harney, *The Way It Is.*)

page 89   "There is no death..." Chief Seattle of the Suquamish to Isaac Stevens of the Washington Territory, 1854. (*See* For Further Reading, Time–Life Books, *American Indians: Spirit World.*)

page 99   "...as much lovingness as though they would give their hearts." From Columbus's journals. (*See* For Further Reading, D. M. Dooling and Paul Jordan–Smith, *I Become Part of It.*)

FOR FURTHER READING

Avery, Susan, and Linda Skinner. *Extraordinary American Indians.* Chicago: Children's Press, 1992.

Dooling, D. M., and Paul Jordan–Smith. *I Become Part of It: Sacred Dimensions in Native American Life.* San Francisco: HarperCollins, 1989.

Harney, Corbin. *The Way It Is.* Nevada City, Calif.: Blue Dolphin Publishing, 1995.

Hirschfelder, Arlene. *Happily May I Walk: American Indians and Alaska Natives Today.* New York: Charles Scribners Sons, 1986.

Hirschfelder, Arlene, and Paulette Molin. *The Encyclopedia of Native American Religions.* New York: Facts On File, 1992.

Monroe, Jean Guard, and Ray A. Williamson. *First Houses.* Boston: Houghton Mifflin, 1993.

Time–Life Books, *American Indians: Spirit World.* Alexandria, Va., 1992.

Time–Life Books, *American Indians: Cycles of Life.* Alexandria, Va., 1994.

Verslius, Arthur. *Native American Traditions.* Shaftsbury, Dorset, England, and Rockport, Mass.: Element Books, 1994.

Walker, Paul Robert. *American Indian Lives: Spiritual Leaders.* New York: Facts On File, 1994.

INDEX

The letter *p* denotes a photo.

Alaska, 13, 14, 67
Algonquin, 31, 74, 75; guardian spirits, 31; Medicine Lodge tradition, 74–75
Allah, 16
"Amazing Grace" translations, 100
American Indian Movement (AIM), 113
American Indian Religious Freedom Act of 1978 (AIRFA), 107, 114
American Indian Religious Freedom Amendment of 1994, 114
Animal spirits, 19, 21, 26; Buffalo Calf Woman, 6, 21, 26; and power of birds, 21; Raven, 19, 21. *See also* Coyote; Eagle.
Animism, 13
Anishinabe, 20, 71
Apache, 25; puberty rite, 84–86; and taboos, 85; tipi, 84; White Painted Woman, 84
Arapaho, Offerings Lodge, 57
Arizona, 70, 97

Basketry, 15
Bering Strait, 13
Bible, 11, 34, 119
Big Foot, Chief, 106
Bighorn Mountains, 23, *p23*
Black Elk, 45, *p45*, 68
Blanca Peak, 37
Blue Lake, 117
Born for Water, 38
Buddha, 11, 34
Buddhism, 23, 34
Buffalo, role of, 44–45, 46
Buffalo Calf Woman, 6, 21, 26, 44, 46, 82
Buffalo People, 26, 45, 46
Buffalo Spirit, 19

California, 20, 39, 57, 98, 103, 104
Canada, 14, 29, 35, 102, 113, 115, 117
Canku Luta. See Lakota (sacred pipe).
Canyon de Chelly National Monument, *p17*, 18
Carlisle Indian School, 104
Carson National Forest, 117
Carter, President Jimmy, 114
Changing Woman, 37–38, 86
Chantways, Navajo, 72, 73–74, 86;

Beadways, 73; Blessingway, 73, 86; Earthway, 73; Nightway, 73; Shootingway, 73; Windway, 73
Charles V, 95
Cherokee, 14, 21; "Amazing Grace" translation, 100; cause of illness, 66; healing herbs, 75; relocation, 99
Cheyenne, and New Life Lodge, 57
Chicasaw relocation, 99
Childhood rituals, Hopi, 83; Lakota, 82–83; Navajo, 81; Tewa, 83
Chilocco Indian School, 104
Chilula shamans, 27
China, 14
Choctaw, "Amazing Grace" translation, 100; relocation, 99
Christianity, "Amazing Grace" translations, 100; Baptist, 100; and Indian Shaker Church, 102–103; and Iroquois, 98–99; Jesuits, 98; and Longhouse Religion, 99; missionary efforts, 95–98; and Native American Church, 106–107; Pima, 96; Popé's revolt, 96; Quakers, 98; and Seminole, 99–101; Slocum, John, 102–103; and Tohono O'odham, 96
Chumash, and role of sun, 20
Clinton, President Bill, 114
Colorado, 14
Columbia River, 42
Columbus, Christopher, 94
Confucianism, 13
Corn dances, 59–61
Corn Spirit, 19
Cornplanter, Chief, 98
Costumes, 50–51, 52–53
Courts of Indian Offenses, 102
Coyote, 19, 42
Creator, names for, 18–19
Creek, 99, 100; "Amazing Grace" translation, 100; relocation, 99
Crow, 22; sun dance, 57; Thirst Lodge, 57
Culture Hero, 18, 39

Dance, 13, 29; animal dances, 51–52; buffalo dance, 52, 60; circle dance, 48; corn dances, 59–61; creation beliefs and, 48; eagle dance, 52; feather dance, 60; Gazing at the Sun, 57; Green Corn Dance, 59–60, 101; Hopi, *p49*, 50; Inuit, 48;

Kwakiutl, 50; Lakota, 57–58; Line Dance, 48; Long Dance, 60; Pueblo, 50; Pueblo Corn Dance, 61; purpose of, 48–50; Ribbon Dance, 60; Santa Clara Pueblo, 60, *p60*; Shoshone, 58–59; snake dance, 63; solo dance, 48; Stomp Dance, 59, 60; Sun Dance, 57–62, 102, 110; Teton Sioux, 58
Death, 89–91; Navajo, 90; Ojibwa, 89–90; Winnebago, 90; Wintu, 90
Delaware (Lenape) shamans, 75
Diyin Diné ("Holy People"), 37–38
Drama, 48
Dreams, and Sacred Way, 12
Drumming, 13, 26, 29, 54

Eagle, symbol and role, 30, 119
Eagle Rock, Nevada, 77
Earth Starter, 18, 39
Emergence tales, Coyote, 42; Haida, 40–41; Inuit, 40–41; Iroquois, 35–37; Maidu, 39; Navajo, 37–38; Paiute, 42; Shoshone, 42
Encomienda (colonial system of forced labor), 95
England, 94
Environmental movement, 114
European explorers, 92
Everglades, 99

Fasting, 18
Father Sky, 72
First Man, 18
First People, 14, 20
First Woman, 18
Florida, 99, 101
France, 26–27, 94

Gan, 25, 84, 85
Geographical features, formation of, 42–44
Georgia, 99
Ghost Dance religion, 104–106
Ghost Keeping Ceremony (Wanagi Yuhapi), 44
Ghost Shirt, 106
Girl's Puberty Rite (Isnati Awicalowan), 44
Great Lakes, 35
Great Mystery, 12, 16, 18
Great Power, 12
Great Spirit, 12, 16, 18, 22, 24, 30, 34,

52, 63, 71, 78, 89, 91, 92, 98, 108, 112, 119
Green Corn Dance, 59–60, 101
Guardian Spirits, 28, 29–30

Ha'athali (singer), 73
Haida, 40–41, naming ceremony, 80; Raven, 40
Half-Moon Ceremony, 108
Hanbleceya (Vision Quest), 44
Handsome Lake (Skaniadariio), 98–99
Harney, Corbin, 31, 120
Hesperus Peak, 38
Heyoka (clown), 61–62
Hogan, 74
Hopi, 14, 26; childhood rituals, 83; dance, *p49*, 50; kachinas, 26, 52–53, *p53*, 62; kiva, 62; marriage, 88–89; masks, 26; naming ceremony, *p79*, 80; *Niman*, 63; snake dance, 63; *Wuwuchim*, 62
Hozho (harmony), 73
Hunka Ceremony (Hunkapi, or "making of relatives"), 44, 82
Hunkapi. See Lakota.
Hupa shamans, 27
Huron masks, 26

Illness, causes of, 66; Cherokee view of, 66; and evil spirits, 66; healing herbs, 75–76; healing rituals, 70; Inuit view of, 66; Iroquois view of, 66; Lakota Sweat Lodge Ceremony, 71; medicine societies, 74–75; Navajo chantways, 73–74; and modern medicine, 76–77; and object intrusion, 66; shamans, role of, 66–69; and soul loss, 66
Indian schools, 104
Indian Shaker Church, 102–103
Inikagapi. *See* Sweat Lodge Ceremony.
Inuit, 13, 14; dance, 48, 52; emergence tales, 40–41; guardian spirits, 31; shamans, 29; view of illness, 66
Inuk people, 113
Iroquois, 16; and Handsome Lake, 98–99; and Jesuits, 98; Longhouse Religion, 99; Old Man of the Crow, 40; and Quakers, 98; Sky Woman, 35–36; Tawis-karong, 36–37, 40; Tijus-keha, 35–36; and illness, 66
Islam, 16, 34
Isnati Awicalowan. *See* Girl's Puberty Rite.

Jackson, President Andrew, 99
Japan, 14
Jesuits, 97, 98
Jesus, 11, 103
Jews, 34

Kachinas. *See* Hopi.
Kinaalda (puberty rite), 86
Kiowa, 58; "Amazing Grace" translation, 100
Kiva, 62, 83, 96
Klickitats, 42
Koran, 11, 34
Koshare (spirit beings), 61
Kurena (spirit beings), 61
Kusku, 39
Kwakiutl, dance, 50; naming ceremony, 80

Lakota, 16; bear power, 71; Black Elk, 45, *p45*; buffalo, 44–45; Buffalo Calf Woman, 6, 21, 26, 44, 46, 82; *Canku Luta*, 44, 82; childhood rituals, 82; Dance Gazing at the Sun, 57–58; Ghost Keeping Ceremony, 44; Ghost Shirt, 106; Girl's Puberty Rite, 44; healing ceremony, 71–73; *heyoka*, 61–62; *Hunkapi* (making of relatives ceremony), 82, 121; Kiowa belief, 58; *Mitakuye' Oyasin* (chant), 72; puberty rites, 86–88; sacred music, 53–54; sacred pipe, 26, 44–47, 69, *p69*; seven sacred rites, 44; shamans, 27, 69; Sitting Bull, 106; Sun Dance, 6, 64, 82; Sweat Lodge Ceremony, 44, 56, *p56*, 57, 58, 71; Throwing the Ball Ceremony, 44; vision quest, 44; Wakan Tanka, 44, 54; *wapiye' win*, 27; world renewal ceremony, 57
Languages, 10
Lenape (Delaware) medicine men/women, 75
Longhouse Religion, 99
Loo-Wit, 43
Luiseño, 43

Maidu, Earth Starter, 39; Kusku, 39; Morning-Star Woman, 39; Pehi-ipe, 39; Turtle, 39
Maize, 21, 38
Mandan naming ceremony, 81
Manitou (Great Spirit), 12, 16
Marquette, Jacques, 97–98
Marriage, 88–89

Masks. *See* Costumes.
Massachusetts, 94
Massasoit, 95
Master of Life (Tijus-keha), 35–36
Maturity, 89
Medicine bundle, 24–25, 26, 31, 38
Medicine Lodge tradition, 74–75
Medicine man/woman, 13, 26–29, 66–69, *p67, p69, 70, p70*, 75, 82
Medicine wheel, 23, *p23*
Midewiwin (Grand Medicine Society), 74–75
Migration of Native Americans from Asia, 13
Milky Way, 19
Mission of San Xavier del Bac, 96–97
Mississippi River, 98
Modern era, 112–120
Mohawk and encounters with Canadian army, 113
Monster Slayer, 38
Morning Star, 20
Morning-Star Woman, 39
Moses, 11
Mother Earth, 19, 72, 73, 89, 92
Mount Adams, 43
Mount Hood, 43
Mount Saint Helens, 43
Mount Taylor, 38
Multnomahs, 42
Music, Navajo, 54–55; Pueblo, 54; shamans, 55
Muslims, 34

Naming Ceremony, 78–80, 81. *See also* Haida; Hopi; Kwakiutl; Mandan; Tewa; Zuni.
National Eagle Repository, 119
Native American Church, 106–107, 108
Native American Graves Protection and Repatriation Act of 1990 (NAGPRA), 118
Native American religions, ancestors, 117–118; animism, 13; bans of native religious practices, 101–102; ceremonies and rituals, 13, 48–63; and Christianity, 92–109; comparisons to other religions, 11–12, 16; creator, 18; dance, 48–49; and dreams/visions, 18; emergence tales, 34–38, 40–41; evil spirits, 66; fasting, 18; formation of geographical features, 42–44; Ghost Dance, 104–106; and Great Power, 12;

healing the earth, 76; humor, 13, 61–62; medicine men/women, 13, 26–29; and modern medicine, 76–77; origins, 13–14; path of life, 78–91; power of names, 81; prayer, 31, 63; puberty rituals, 83–88; religions today, 110–120; sacred way, 12, 16–31; shamans, 13, 26–29; similarities between tribes, 13; storytelling, 32–47; supernatural beings of creation, 34–37; wholeness and healing, 64–77; work, 14. *See also* Indian Shaker Church; Longhouse Religion; Native American Church; Oral tradition; Spirit world.

Native American Religious Purposes Permit, 119

Navajo, Blanca Peak, 37; Changing Woman, 37–38, 86; chantways, 72, 73–74; childhood rituals, 81; Coyote, 42; death ritual, 90; *Diyin Diné*, 37–38; First Man/Woman, 18, 37; First People, 14, 37–38; *ha'athali*, 73; Hesperus Peak, 38; *hogan*, 74; *hozho*, 73; kachinas, 83; kinaalda, 86; kiva, 83; maize, 38; medicine bundle, 25, 38; Monster Slayer, 38; Mount Taylor, 38; music, 54–55; puberty rites, 84, 86; ritual sand paintings, 73; sacred land, 24; sky spirits, 20; Spider Woman, 18; Talking God, 37; White Shell Woman, 38; yei, 73, 74

Nevada, 77, 104

New Life Lodge, 57

New Mexico, 55, 60, p93, 94

Niman (Hopi ceremony), 63

Nisqually and formation of geographical features, 42, 43

Nixon, President Richard, 117

North Dakota, 104

Northern Paiute Ghost Dance, 104, 105

Nova Scotia, 35

Object intrusion, 66, 71

Offerings Lodge, 57

Ojibwa, 19; death ritual, 89–90; Midewiwin (Grand Medicine Society), 74–75; shamans, 29; vision quest, 30

Oklahoma, 99, 104

Oral tradition, creation stories, 34; cycles of stories, 34; emergence tales, 37–38, 39; formation of geographical features, 42–44; Iroquois, 35–37; Klickitats, 42; Lakota, 44–46; Maidu, 39; Mount Adams, 43; Mount Hood, 43; Mount Saint Helens, 43; Multnomahs, 42; Navajo, 37–38; Nisqually, 42; sacred pipe of Lakota, 44–47; trickster tales, 39–42

Oregon, 114

Orenda (Great Spirit), 12, 16

Origins of Native American religions, 13–14

Paho (prayer sticks), 26

Paiute, 42

Papago Indian Reservation (Tohono O'odham), 97

Path of Life, 78–91

Pawnee creation story, 20

Pehi-ipe, 39

Pennsylvania, 104

Penobscot, 26

Personate, 50

Peyote, 114; Half-Moon Ceremony (Tipi Way), 108; ritual, 107–108; Quanah Parker (Kiowa) Way, 108

Picuris Pueblo, New Mexico, p93, 94

Pilgrims, 94–95

Pima and Christianity, 96

Pine Ridge Indian Reservation, 70

Pipe ceremonies of Lakota. *See* Lakota.

Plant spirits, 21–22, 75; tobacco, 22

Poeh (Tewa path of life), 80

Pope, 96

Population in 1600, 10; population today, 14

Potlatch, 80, 102

Powwows, 15, p15

Puberty Rites, Apache, 84–86; Lakota, 86–88; Navajo, 86

Pueblo, bear power, 71; buffalo dance, 52; corn dance, 50, 61; costumes, 50; guardian spirit, 29; kiva, 96; Koshare, 61; Kurena, 61; paho, 26; Popé and the revolt, 96; Santa Clara Pueblo, 55, 60; songs, 54; world renewal ceremony, 57

Quakers, 98

Quanah Parker, Chief, 108, 109, p109

Quebec, 113

Raven, 19, 21, 40–41

Red Weasel, 53

Religious Freedom Restoration Act of 1993, 114

Relocation, 99

Reservation system, 101

Ritual year, and renewal of the Earth, 62–63

Rock Creek Canyon, Nevada, 77

Roman Catholic missionaries, 95–99

Roosevelt, President Theodore, 117

Sacred clowns, 61–62, 81

Sacred land, 116–117

Sacred music, 53–55

Sacred Way, 12, 14–15, 16–31

San Francisco Peaks, 38

Sand painting, 73–74

Santa Clara Pueblo, 55, 60

Santa Fe, New Mexico, 94

Seattle, Chief, 89

Secular age, 4

Seminole, Baptist churches, 100–101; buffalo dance, 60; and Christianity, 99–101; feather dance, 60; Green Corn Dance, 59–60, 101; Long Dance, 60; Osceola, 99; relocation, 99; Ribbon Dance, 60; scratching ceremony, 60; Stomp Dance, 60, 100; world renewal ceremony, 57

Seneca, 98

Serra, Father Junipero, 98

Shaman, abilities and training, 27–29; bear power, 71; guardian spirit helpers, 28, 29–30; and John Slocum, 103; music, 55; role, 13, 84; role with illness, 66–69; taboos, 31

Shasta, 27

Shinto, 11, 14

Shoshone, 42; and Christianity, 102; Eagle Rock, 77; medicine man, p65, 66; Sun Dance, 57, 58–59; Sweat Lodge Ceremony, 77; Thirst Lodge, 57; world renewal ceremonies, 57

Siberia, 13

Sioux peoples, 44, 46. *See also* Lakota.

Sitting Bull, Chief, 106

Skaniadariio (Handsome Lake), 98–99

Sky Woman, 35–36

Slocum, John, 102–103

Snake Dance, 63

Society of Friends (Quakers), 98

Soul Loss, 66

South Dakota, 70

Spain, 94, 95, 96, 98, 99

Speaking Rock, p17, 18

Spider Rock, p17, 18

Spider Woman, 18
Spirit World, 16–31; animal spirits, 19, 21; atmosphere beings, 19; guardian spirits, 28, 29–30; interaction with, 24; medicine wheels, 23, *p23*; plant spirits, 19, 21–22; power of prayer, 31; sacred objects, 24–26; shamans, 26–29; sky spirits, 19–20; spirit in places, 22–24; and taboos, 31; underworld spirits, 19. *See also* Gan.
Sun Dance, 6, 20, 62, 102, 110
Supreme Court of United States, 114, 117
Suquamish, 89
Sweat Lodge Ceremony (Inikagapi). *See* Lakota.

Taboos, 31, 85
Talking God, 37
Taoism, 11, 13, 16
Taos, New Mexico, 94
Taos people, 116–117
Tapa Wankayeyapi (Throwing the Ball Ceremony), 44
Tawis-karong, 36–37, 40
Tennessee Valley, 117
Teton Sioux, 19, 44, 58
Tewa, childhood rituals, 83; naming ceremony, 80; *poeh* (path of life), 80; sand paintings, 80; water pouring ritual, 83

Thirst Lodge, 57
Throwing the Ball Ceremony (Tapa Wankayeyapi), 44
Thunderbird, 19
Tijus-keha, 35–36
Tlingit and Raven, 21
Tobacco, 22
Tohono O'odham, 70, 97; and Christianity, 96, 97
Traditional homes, 8–9
Trail of Tears, 99
Treviño, Juan, 96
Tribal membership, 14
Trickster tales, Coyote, 42; Iroquois, 40; Old Man of the Crow, 40; Raven, 40–41; Tawis-karong, 40
Tuscon, Arizona, 97

Umatilla, 14
United States Bureau of Indian Affairs, 102

Vision quests, 30, 44, 55

Wakan Tanka. See Great Spirit.
Walker River, Nevada, 104
Wampanoags, 95
Wanagi Yuhapi (Ghost Keeping Ceremony), 44
Wapiye' win (spirit-calling woman), 27
Washington, 14, 103
White Mountain Apache, 25, *p25*

White Painted Woman, 84
White Shell Woman, (Changing Woman), 38
Wind River Reservation, Wyoming, 66
Winnebago mourning ritual, 90
Wintu song for the dead, 90
Wodziwob, 105
World renewal ceremonies, 57, 64
World-Maker, 18
Wounded Knee Massacre, 106
Wovoka, 105, 106
Wuwuchim (Hopi ceremony), 62
Wyoming, 23, 66

Yakima, 18
Yei (Navajo holy people), 73, 74

Zuni, 20; naming ceremony, 80; *paho*, 26; Twin War God fetishes, 118–119